SUCCESSFUL BANK ASSET/LIABILITY MANAGEMENT

A guide to the future beyond gap

John W. Bitner
with
Robert A. Goddard

John Wiley & Sons, Inc.

New York • Chichester • Brisbane • Toronto • Singapore

In recognition of the importance of preserving what has been written, it is a policy of John Wiley & Sons, Inc. to have books of enduring value published in the United States printed on acid-free paper, and we exert our best efforts to that end.

This publication is designed to provide accurate and authoritative information in regard to the subject matter covered. It is sold with the understanding that the publisher is not engaged in rendering legal, accounting, or other professional services. If legal advice or other expert assistance is required, the services of a competent professional person should be sought. *From a Declaration of Principles jointly adopted by a Committee of the American Bar Association and a Committee of Publishers.*

Library of Congress Cataloging-in-Publication Data

Bitner, John W., 1948–
   Successful bank asset/liability management : a guide to the future
beyond Gap / by John W. Bitner with Robert A. Goddard.
      p.   cm.
   Includes index.
   ISBN 0-471-52731-9 (cloth)
   1. Asset-liability management (Banking)   I. Goddard, Robert A.
II. Title.
HG1615.25.B57   1992
332.1'068'1—dc20   91-41363

Printed and bound in the United States of America by Braun-Brumfield, Inc.

10 9 8 7 6 5 4 3 2 1

This book is lovingly dedicated to our parents; John W. and Gertrude B. Bitner, and Alvan R. and Barbara A. Goddard.

—John and Bob

To my wife Patricia, and to Christopher and Merideth, with all my love.

—Bob

Acknowledgments

This book is a guide to implementing a successful asset/liability (A/L) management process in commercial banks and thrift institutions. The first portion of the book provides guidance to financial institutions that are in the early stages of implementing asset/liability management in their organizations. It provides detailed information on forming an A/L committee, developing a policy, and selecting a simulation model. The focus of the remaining chapters is on more advanced topics associated with successful strategies of asset/liability management. This section addresses the subject of identifying, measuring, and managing interest rate risks.

The primary audience for this guide is A/L managers and members of the A/L management committee. It also serves as an important reference for Boards of Directors; regulatory authorities; finance departments of colleges and universities; and consulting and accounting professionals.

We thank the many people who contributed in the preparation of the manuscript, especially Christine Danjou, Cathy Sullivan, Kathy Mills, and Mildred Reeves. We would also like to acknowledge Helene Ullenes for her assistance in editing early drafts of several chapters.

We are especially grateful to our editor Wendy Grau. Her guidance during the planning and writing of this book was instrumental to the completion of the project. We greatly appreciate her patience and support.

We also express our gratitude to our colleagues at Eastern Bank for their support and encouragement in this endeavor.

Finally, we would like to acknowledge the following individuals who provided opportunities for our professional growth and development, each of whom has served as a mentor at various stages in our careers: Louis Attardo, Howard Baldwin, Philip Duddy, Glen Fenstermacher, Cyril Jemson, and Stanley Lukowski.

John W. Bitner
Robert A. Goddard

Contents

Contents

Contents

1

Introduction: Evolution of
Interest Rate Risk Management

The first major bank regulations were legislated after the "banking holiday" in 1933 to ensure that a major banking crisis would not be repeated. The legislation created the Federal Reserve System and the Federal Deposit Insurance Corporation to manage the regulatory process. The regulatory restrictions on the banks greatly reduced many of the risks in the banking industry. Deposits were taken in at mandated rates and loaned out at legally established higher rates. Therefore, the rates remained unaffected by market pressures. To those outside the banking industry, the phrase "3-6-3" became a common reference about bankers. Bankers would bring in deposits at 3%, lend the funds at 6%, and be home for the day by 3:00 P.M.

The regulated banking environment created a tranquil and stable period for the industry. However, rising interest rates in the early 1970s forced financial institutions, for the first time since the 1920s, into a competitive market environment. For years, Regulation "Q" had controlled the rates financial institutions could pay on deposits. In 1973, Regulation Q was amended so banks could compete with deposit alternatives as long as the size of the deposit exceeded $100,000. This provided some relief from the disintermediation occurring when bank customers used deposit dollars to purchase high-yielding securities not subject to the rate restrictions of Regulation Q. However, commercial banks and thrift institutions continued to lobby Congress for the right to compete freely in the financial markets for deposit dollars by offering competitive market interest rates on all types of deposits. Eventually, they achieved their objective when Regulation Q began to be phased out in 1978. By 1981, Regulation Q was completely gone, and banks were, for the first time in decades, permitted to compete freely for deposit dollars. Just when bankers began to offer competitive market rates of interest on their deposits, the U.S. economy experienced a sharp acceleration in the rate of inflation. The Federal Reserve responded to the sharply higher inflation by forcing interest rates to their highest level in this century. This action on the part of the Federal Reserve Bank quickly drove banks' cost of funds to record-high levels.

Unlike the bank failures of the 1990s, most of which were caused by credit problems, bank failures during the late 1970s and early 1980s were mostly the result of poorly managed interest rate risk. Many financial institutions funded long-term fixed-rate assets with short-term liabilities. As long as deposit and loan rates remained regulated, this funding mismatch was not a problem. However, when interest rates moved sharply higher during the early 1980s, the consequences of the mismatched interest rate sensitivity became obvious. Financial institutions that had been generating profits for decades soon began to produce substantial losses.

Years of regulation had made it unnecessary to develop the discipline of interest rate risk management. Therefore, the deregulation of the banking system caught many bankers unprepared to manage the interest rate risk to which their institutions were suddenly exposed. Only the largest and most sophisticated banks had developed in-house, mainframe applications that were able to identify and measure the interest rate risk inherent in their balance sheet. Relatively few financial institutions were able to measure their interest rate risk exposure and the impact of that exposure on their net interest margin as interest rates changed. However, they soon understood that being liability sensitive when the prime rate approached 20% caused a severe compression in earnings.

Many savings and loan and thrift institutions were particularly devastated by the sharp increase in interest rates. Their balance sheets consisted primarily of 30-year fixed-rate mortgages funded by short-term deposits. As interest rates began to rise, many institutions failed to address the massive interest rate risk inherent in their balance sheet. They did not have an interest rate risk management process in place and they failed to believe interest rates would increase to the levels eventually reached in the early 1980s. For example, the management of First Pennsylvania Bank in Philadelphia was convinced interest rates had reached a long-term secular peak in 1976 when the ten-year Treasury note yield reached 8%. To lock in the rates, they quickly extended the average maturity of their asset structure. As Treasury note rates moved into double digits the bank began to produce massive losses, which eventually caused its demise. The more capital a financial institution had, the better it was able to reduce its interest rate risk exposure by selling long-term fixed rate assets at substantial losses. Consequently, those institutions with strong capital positions survived while many of the lesser-capitalized institutions failed.

Banks referred to the interest rate timing difference between their assets and their liabilities as the "gap" position. If a bank had more liabilities repricing in any given period than it had assets repricing in the same period, it referred to its gap position as negative, or liability sensitive. If more assets repriced in any given period than liabilities, the bank's gap position was referred to as being positive or asset sensitive. The general assumption of the regulators and senior bank management was that matching the timing of the interest rate changes on assets and liabilities would eliminate the interest rate risk. However, they began to discover that the banks' gap positions could not completely explain the change in the net interest margin for a given change in interest rates. Clearly, there were forms of interest rate risk present in the banks' balance sheet structure other than gap.

Academics and Wall Street analysts began to identify other more subtle yet substantial forms of interest rate risk such as basis risk (the risk that different interest rates will not change by the same magnitude within a given period of time), and the impact of embedded options (loan payoffs and early deposit withdrawals). As their research progressed, they realized that to measure the various forms of interest rate risk to which a bank was exposed required much more than a simple gap analysis. Aggressive banks took advantage of the advent of the personal computer to develop software that could measure the impact of the various forms of interest rate risk by modeling the bank and testing its performance under various interest rate scenarios. These models provided banks with a powerful tool to identify, measure, and manage their total interest rate risk.

As bankers became accustomed to modeling the impact of interest rate changes on their net interest income, they began to think of their institution's balance sheet as a portfolio of fixed-rate assets being funded by a portfolio of fixed-rate liabilities. This concept was reinforced by many Wall Street firms, which created procedures to turn heretofore totally illiquid loans into marketable securities and developed markets in which bank CDs could be actively traded. These concepts revolutionized the way senior bank management viewed their balance sheet structure and resulted in effective new methods with which banks could manage interest rate risk exposure.

As more of the bank's balance sheet began to be regarded as a portfolio of marketable interest-bearing securities, it was inevitable that models would be developed that would calculate the market value of the assets and the market value of the liabilities to determine the true net worth of the financial institution. The record number of bank failures in the early 1990s has accelerated this development as regulators want to determine a financial institution's true net worth or liquidation value.

The science of asset/liability management has evolved very rapidly since the early 1980s. For this reason, the degree to which banks use the asset/liability management process varies widely. Some banks use the latest sophisticated modeling systems to estimate the impact various strategies and interest rate movements will have on their net interest income and the net value of their institution. However, most financial institutions, while having some form of asset/ liability management, do not incorporate recent developments in the field into their management process. These financial institutions usually have established an asset/liability management committee, have written an interest rate risk management policy, and use a simple modeling system to measure the impact on the net interest income of a change in interest rates. However, many of these institutions use simulation models to calculate only their gap position.

Regulators are becoming increasingly concerned about financial institutions that either have no asset/liability management procedures or use a very rudimentary process. New banking regulations are forcing senior management teams that had either been resisting or ignoring asset/liability management procedures to incorporate them in the management of their institutions. The regulations require financial institutions to have a detailed interest rate risk management policy stating their maximum interest rate risk exposure, have in place a formal management process usually in the form of an asset/liability management committee, and use a modeling system sophisticated enough to identify and measure the impact of the various forms of interest rate risk on an institution's earnings and net value.

This book has been designed as a guide for interest rate risk managers with various levels of experience and knowledge in the field. Readers with a more advanced understanding of asset/liability management may want to skip Chapters 2, 3, and 4. However, for institutions just getting started in the asset/liability management process, Chapters 2 through 4 will serve as a guide to organizing an asset/liability management committee, selecting a modeling system, and writing an interest rate risk management policy. Chapters 5 and 6 will examine the fundamental process of asset/liability management, that is, identifying, measuring, and managing interest rate risk. Interest rate forecasting techniques and the ability to conduct a critical self-analysis are important to successful asset/liability management and are discussed in Chapters 7 and 8. The final chapters provide the framework for putting the asset/liability management process into action with insight and advice from leading practitioners in the field.

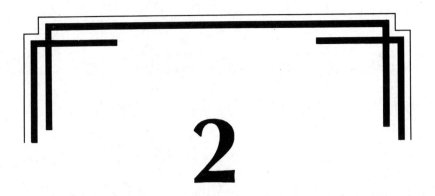

2

Forming an Asset/Liability Committee

The most important element when beginning the asset/ liability (A/L) management process is to have the total support of the chief executive officer. The CEO's support should be a clear indication to all the departments of the organization to cooperate with the asset/liability manager in establishing and maintaining the asset/liability management process. It is necessary to have the cooperation of all the departments because almost every area of the organization will be involved in the process. The accounting department must supply a constant flow of current and historical data to the asset/liability modeling system. The marketing department is used to design new products and encourage customers to use certain existing products that are consistent with the committee's objectives. The investment department's actions, as well as the pricing of loan and deposit products, must be coordinated with the interest rate risk and liquidity objectives of the asset/liability committee (ALCO). Because asset/liability management addresses the risks inherent in the balance sheet, every area of the organization is involved in the process.

The CEO's support must be more than tacit permission to begin the development of an A/L management process. The CEO must designate A/L management as a high priority objective and clearly communicate that message to every level of management within the institution. It will be difficult for the asset/liability manager to successfully carry out the strategies of the ALCO without the full cooperation of all areas in the organization.

If the CEO is not going to assume responsibility for the A/L management process, a senior manager should be designated as the A/L manager. The A/L manager will be responsible for implementing, maintaining, and improving the A/L management process of the organization. When stating the institution's commitment to the A/L management process, the CEO should name the A/L manager so the entire management team is clear about who is managing the process.

A good candidate for the A/L manager would be a senior executive thoroughly familiar with finance and, in particular, interest rate theory. Asset/liability management involves viewing the balance sheet as a very complex interest rate arbitrage where funds are obtained from many sources at various interest rates and employed in a wide variety of assets at rates high enough to cover the interest paid on the liabilities and the operating expenses and produce a profit. Inherent in this process are many forms of credit, liquidity, and interest rate risks that must be understood by the A/L manager. For this reason, the institution's chief financial officer or the chief investment officer is frequently selected as the A/L manager.

The first action of the A/L manager should be to appoint the members of the ALCO. The committee must be large enough to include the major areas of the organization that will be most heavily involved in the A/L management process, but not be so large that it becomes difficult to function effectively. Ideally, the committee should consist of at least four members but not exceed eight members. The structure of the committee can vary but will generally include the chief executive officer, the chief financial officer, the senior officer responsible for the lending functions, the senior officer responsible for deposit activity, and the senior investment officer (see Figure 2.1). It is very important to have at least one person on the committee who is thoroughly knowledgeable about the institution's financial data. The

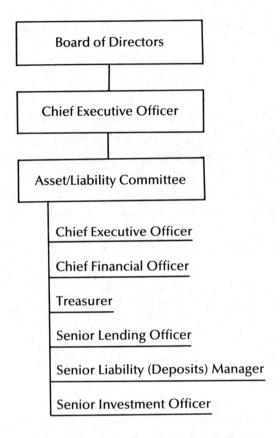

Figure 2.1 Asset/liability management structure

ALCO will be making major decisions based on the data entered into the simulation model and other reports supplied by the accounting department. If the model operator is not properly entering the institution's data into the model, or someone in the accounting department is incorrectly reporting financial information to the committee, there must be at least one, and preferably several, members of the ALCO who understand the institution's financial data well enough to detect the error before the data is used to make decisions.

The first task of the asset/liability management committee is to define its role within the organization. The definition should be clear, concise and encompass the total activity of the asset/liability management process. Managing the various forms of complex and constantly changing interest rate risks and providing for an institution's liquidity needs is an enormous responsibility. The magnitude and complexity of the asset/liability management process can at times seem overwhelming to the ALCO members and provides plenty of opportunity for the committee to lose its focus and concentrate too much on one function or area of the organization. A concise, comprehensive, clearly stated role definition for the ALCO will provide a framework within which the activities of the ALCO can be carried out and will provide a balanced focus that will help prevent the ALCO members from feeling overwhelmed. An example of a well-constructed statement is as follows:

> The asset/liability management function involves planning, directing, and controlling the flow, level, mix, cost, and yield of the consolidated funds of the corporation. These responsibilities are interwoven with the overall objectives of achieving the corporation's financial goals and controlling financial risks.

After defining the purpose of the asset/liability management process within the organization, the committee must establish some general goals. The goals are statements about what the organization proposes to accomplish. A goal statement identifies the key variables that should be the focus and criteria for management decisions. The statement must be broad enough to allow for flexibility yet confined to areas deemed to be of essential importance to the firm. The goal statement should include only a few general goals and be consistent with the ALCO's statement of general purpose. An example of a set of goals is:

1. Keep the level of interest rate risk within stated limits.
2. Enhance the corporation's net interest income.
3. Provide adequate liquidity to the corporation.

Defining the role of the asset/liability management function and stating the committee's general goals not only provides a clearly stated base for future asset/liability management actions, but also forms the beginning of the asset/liability management policy.

Writing an asset/liability management policy and submitting it to the board of directors for their approval should be an early priority of the ALCO. During the first few meetings of the ALCO, members must address fundamental questions such as:

How can we measure interest rate risk?

How much interest rate risk can the institution tolerate?

What constitutes liquidity?

How much liquidity is enough?

As the ALCO members discuss these questions, the conclusions they reach will form the basis from which the asset/

liability management policy can be developed. The issues these questions raise are complex and require a solid understanding of the asset/liability management process. Institutions may discover that the members of their ALCO do not have the training or experience to confidently answer these questions. A top priority for these institutions should be to quickly educate their ALCO members about asset/liability management. Attending courses and seminars offered by the various banking associations and model vendors and carefully reading the books and numerous articles about A/L management are the primary sources of education. Those institutions that do not want to wait for their ALCO members to become educated before beginning the process may want to hire an outside consultant to assist in establishing or improving the A/L management process in their institution. The consultant not only brings experience and knowledge to the ALCO, but can serve as a tutor to teach the ALCO members about A/L management.

Other questions the ALCO members must ask when beginning the asset/liability management process are:

What information is required to make strategic asset/liability management decisions?

What tools are required to provide the information?

How is the information most clearly presented?

Part of the answer to these questions is a trial-and-error process. Reports that are useful to the committee will continue to be used while those that are not useful will be discontinued. However, much time can be saved by drawing upon the experience of other institutions.

At most institutions, the single most important tool in the asset/liability management process is a sophisticated computer simulation model. Gap reports and various types of matrix analysis can isolate and broadly measure certain types of interest rate risk. But only a computer simulation model can measure the full impact of the various forms of interest rate risk on an institution's earnings and net value. There are a wide variety of models currently available. They range from a very basic model costing a few thousand dollars to complex models costing $75,000 or more.

One of the primary considerations when selecting a model is that it is able to produce the reports required by the ALCO. Most models will produce a balance sheet, income statement, and gap reports. However, not all models can present the information on graphs, produce cash flows, or calculate the net value of portfolio equity. If the ALCO prefers to see the information presented graphically, use cash flow reports to project liquidity positions, and requires the net value of portfolio equity to be calculated, it is important to restrict the search for an A/L model to those that offer these features.

It is also important to know how the model will be used. Strategic planning requires extended time horizons to test the impact of long-term plans. If the model is to be used as a strategic planning tool, the model must be capable of projecting the data on a five-year time horizon. The model must also have the ability to alter the balance sheet composition in future periods. This will enable the A/L manager to model test long-term strategic plans for changing the composition of the asset structure or the mix of funding liabilities. However, if the model is to be used in a defensive manner, a twelve-month time horizon and the ability to test various interest rate scenarios may be sufficient.

The scope and complexity of the asset/liability management process requires that detailed information about the institution's liquidity, capital position, and interest rate risk exposure be made available to members of the ALCO. The standard report package (see Figure 2.2) should be distributed to the members of the ALCO well in advance of the meeting date. This will provide the members an opportunity to analyze the information and come to the meeting prepared to propose and discuss various strategies to improve the institution's net interest income.

The primary functions of the ALCO are to provide adequate liquidity to the institution, manage the interest rate risk within set limits, and maintain and enhance the institution's capital position. Rather than spend time discussing each of the reports in the standard report package, many institutions summarize the information according to the three primary functions of the committee and place the summary on top of the individual reports. At the ALCO meeting the summary statements are carefully reviewed and discussed with the individual reports used to explore possible strategies or understand in greater detail a particular element or trend in the institution's financial structure. The following is a typical example of the summary statements.

Liquidity

The Bank's liquidity position is strong. The projected liquidity needs for the next six months indicate the net cash flow will supply $xx million of additional liquid funds. In the event of

Summary	Liquidity Position
Statements	Interest Rate Risk
	Capital Position
Liquidity	Cash flow analysis (Table 8.6)
Analyses	Sources of liquidity (Table 8.7)
	Projected liquidity requirement (Table 8.8)
	Total borrowing positions
	Total loan commitments outstanding
Interest Rate	Interest rate forecast (Figure 2.3)
Risk Analyses	Recent history of interest rate movements
	Dynamic balance sheet analysis
	Periodic GAP reports (Table 5.13)
	Cumulative GAP reports (Table 5.13)
	Dynamic income statement
	Rates up 300 basis points
	Rates unchanged
	Rates down 300 basis points
	Dynamic simulation results (Figure 5.4)
	List of model assumptions
	Current status of interest rate risk hedges
	(i.e., swaps, caps, floors)
	Analysis of the net value of portfolio equity
Capital	Core (leverage) capital analysis
Analyses	Risk-based capital analysis

Figure 2.2 Standard reports for ALCO meetings

an unexpected permanent shift in the Bank's liquidity requirements, $xxx million is available to meet the need from the
sale of assets ($xxx of which can be supplied with little or no
loss of principal).

Interest Rate Risk

Despite the Bank's $xxx million one-year liability-sensitive
gap position, the Bank remains exposed to compression in

the net interest margin during a sustained sharp decline in interest rates. The compression is the result of the normal basis shift that occurs between time deposit and lending rates as interest rates decline. However, it is the ALCO's opinion that rates are near their lowest levels for the current business cycle. Therefore, the ALCO has reversed its previous strategy and is now encouraging depositors to extend deposit maturities and is promoting floating rate loans, both of which will reduce the Bank's liability-sensitive gap position. Also, the use of interest rate swaps is being explored as a means of accelerating the process.

Capital Position

The capital position of the corporation is sufficient to meet all regulatory requirements. The traditionally computed capital position of the corporation is currently x.xx%. The corporation's tier 1 capital ratio is x.xx%, and the tier 2 capital ratio is x.xx%. The regulator's minimum risk-adjusted capital requirement is 8.00%. The traditionally computed minimum capital requirement is 4.00%.

The detailed reports supporting the liquidity summary statement are; the cash flow analysis, the sources of liquidity report and the projected liquidity requirement (see Tables 8.6, 8.7, and 8.8). These reports provide detailed information about the institution's future liquidity requirements and its ability to satisfy the requirements. The projected cash flow analysis should be reviewed each quarter by the ALCO. If the actual changes in total loans and deposits do not correlate well with the projected changes, the ALCO must determine whether it is a brief onetime occurrence, a shift in seasonal trends, or a structural change developing in the institution's balance sheet. When the ALCO discovers a change in loan or deposit trends, the A/L manager must adjust the simulation model to reflect the new trends.

Other information that may be helpful in understanding the available liquidity and future liquidity requirements is provided in the total borrowings report and the report of total loan commitments outstanding. The total borrowings position report is a list of all current borrowing positions categorized by type of borrowing, such as federal funds purchased and reverse repurchase agreements outstanding, and lists the amount, rate, and maturity of each borrowing position. The report enables the ALCO to monitor the total amount of outstanding debt and alerts the committee to upcoming loan maturities. If the institution is in sound financial condition, the maturing borrowings can easily be renewed. However, if the institution's financial quality has deteriorated since the loans were first advanced, the lenders may be unwilling to renew the loans. If the institution is unable to refinance the loans with other lenders, the maturing loans will create a need for additional liquidity to pay off the loans. The ALCO must be aware of the need for liquidity, which can occur due to a liquidity crunch in the credit markets or changes in the institution's financial condition.

The total loan commitments outstanding report lists the total amount by loan type of the loans to which the institution has committed but not yet funded. A surge in loan commitments will give the asset/liability manager an early warning of a future drain on the institution's liquidity position. Conversely, a sudden decline in loan commitments will provide advance notice of an increase in the liquidity position. If the loan commitments decline during a period when the rates on alternative investments are low, the report will enable the ALCO to take action to prevent an excessive liquidity accumulation. One action the ALCO could take is to lower deposit rates. This action benefits the institution in two ways. It reduces the institution's average cost of funds and prevents the accumulation of excess liquidity by slowing the growth of deposits or may even cause deposits to decline.

Most simulation models require an interest rate forecast (Figure 2.3). Some managers believe it is impossible to forecast interest rates and simply extend the current rates into the future as their interest rate forecast. However, other managers believe it is possible to anticipate the general direction of interest rates by studying the business cycle and understanding the impact of cyclical pressures in the economy on interest rates (see Chapter 7). For institutions that forecast interest rates, the revised forecast should be presented and discussed at each ALCO meeting. Although the extreme high and low interest rate scenarios may call for defensive action when used in the simulation model, the institution's strategies will be most influenced by the interest rate forecast deemed most likely to occur. For this reason, the ALCO must be sure the interest rate forecast used by the simulation model accurately reflects the committee's opinion about the future direction of interest rates.

To assist the committee in their discussion of the interest rate forecast, the A/L manager may want to provide the committee with current statistics and historical information about the economic factors that exert the most influence on the future course of interest rates. Factors such as changes in the gross domestic product, the index of lending economic indicators, inflation rates, and money supply growth may be considered by the ALCO when they discuss the interest rate

	Current 2/92	1 Month 3/92	2 Months 4/92	3 Months 5/92	4 Months 6/92	5 Months 7/92	6 Months 8/92	7 Months 9/92	8 Months 10/92	9 Months 11/92	10 Months 12/92	11 Months 1/93	12 Months 2/93
Prime rate	6.50	6.25	6.25	6.25	6.25	6.25	6.25	6.25	6.25	6.25	6.25	6.75	6.75
Fed funds	4.00	3.75	3.50	3.50	3.50	3.50	3.50	3.50	3.50	3.50	3.75	3.85	3.95
90 day T-bill	3.93	3.75	3.50	3.50	3.50	3.50	3.50	3.50	3.50	3.50	3.75	3.85	3.95
90 day LIBOR	4.19	3.75	3.50	3.50	3.50	3.50	3.50	3.50	3.50	3.50	3.75	3.85	3.95
180 day T-bill	4.04	3.80	3.60	3.60	3.60	3.60	3.60	3.60	3.60	3.60	3.80	3.90	4.00
1 year T-bill	4.19	4.00	3.90	3.90	3.70	3.70	3.70	3.70	3.70	3.90	4.00	4.10	4.20
2 year T-note	5.11	5.00	4.90	4.75	4.30	4.30	4.30	4.30	4.30	4.75	4.90	5.00	5.05
3 year T-note	5.51	5.20	5.05	4.95	4.75	4.75	4.75	4.75	4.75	4.95	5.10	5.20	5.25
5 year T-note	6.45	6.15	6.00	5.85	5.65	5.65	5.65	5.65	5.65	5.85	6.00	6.10	6.15
10 year T-note	7.30	7.00	6.80	6.50	6.50	6.50	6.50	6.50	6.50	6.80	6.85	6.95	7.00

Figure 2.3 Interest rate forecast as of 2/05/92

23

forecast. It is also helpful to include a series of graphs depicting the recent history of interest rate movements using rates such as the prime rate, various deposit rates, and Treasury bill and note rates. The interest rates with the largest impact on the institution's balance sheet or interest rates used as major driver rates in the simulation model are usually depicted on the graphs. The interest rate graphs help the ALCO members discern the pattern of interest rate movements during past business cycles and illustrate the relative level of interest rates in the current business cycle.

Some institutions also include a graph illustrating the current basis spreads compared to past basis spreads (see Figure 5.2). Basis risk can cause a serious contraction in the net interest margin when it moves against the current balance sheet structure. However, when the basis moves in a favorable manner for the balance sheet structure, it can provide a significant enhancement to the institution's net interest margin. The ALCO members must be aware of the key interest rates affecting the balance sheet and understand the current basis relationships between the primary rates earned by the assets and the rates paid on the liabilities. When designing strategies for altering the asset structure or the liability funding mix, or selecting synthetic instruments such as LIBOR-based swaps, the committee must take the basis relationship into consideration. For example, one-year adjustable-rate mortgages with a rate based on the cost of funds index (COFI) may have a higher rate in the current market than adjustable-rate mortgages (ARMs) using the one-year Treasury bill rate as their index. However, a better long term return may be realized by purchasing the Treasury indexed ARM. Although the COFI mortgages may offer an initial rate advantage, a basis shift in favor of the one-year

Treasury bill–indexed mortgages will cause the Treasury-indexed mortgages to generate a better rate in the long term. That is, if interest rates increase, the increase in the rate earned on the Treasury-based ARM could greatly exceed the increase of the rate earned on the COFI based ARM. By understanding the relationship between COFI rates and one-year Treasury bill rates, the ALCO can select an index for its adjustable-rate mortgages that will provide a more satisfactory long-term return.

Most of the reports required to measure the interest rate risk inherent in the institution's balance sheet structure can be generated by computer simulation models. When selecting a model, the committee must be sure the model is capable of generating the reports needed for the ALCO's standard report package. The clarity of the reports varies widely between the various models. Therefore, the committee must be certain the model they select will produce the reports in a format that is easily understood by the committee members.

The reports generated by the model are based solely on the data entered into the model. To be sure of having reliable reports, the A/L manager must be certain accurate data are being correctly entered into the model. The balance sheet generated by the model is the basis from which the other reports are generated. If the balance sheet is not accurate, none of the other reports will be accurate. As an additional test of the data's integrity, the ALCO members should review the projected balance sheet to be sure it appears reasonable.

The two primary detailed reports supporting the interest rate risk summary statement are the gap report and the dynamic income analysis. Of the two reports, the dynamic income analysis is the most important because it captures all the various forms of interest rate risk while gap illustrates only the timing difference between the repricing of the assets and the liabilities.

Most simulation models are capable of producing gap reports. The gap is a basic measure of the portion of interest rate risk attributed to the interest rate timing difference between the assets and the liabilities in any given period. The two basic types of gap reports are the periodic gap report, and the cumulative gap report (see Table 5.13). The periodic gap examines the institution's gap position in each period while the cumulative gap measures the combined impact of the various periodic gaps. A detailed discussion regarding the construction and use of gap reports is presented in Chapter 5.

The dynamic income statements reflect the impact of various interest rate changes and are vital for measuring interest rate risk. The projected balance sheet structure is used to test several interest rate scenarios. The impact of each interest rate scenario is indicated by the change in the net interest income. The change in the net interest income is the result of the institution's exposure to all forms of interest rate risk. Unlike gap, which measures only the interest rate timing difference between assets and liabilities, the dynamic income statements capture the effects of basis risks and embedded options as well as the interest rate risk created by repricing timing differences. An effective way to present this information to the committee is to plot the net income figures produced by the various interest rate scenarios on a single graph (see Figure 5.4). If any of the scenarios cause the net interest income to move below the lowest acceptable limit for the net interest income, the ALCO should consider taking corrective action.

To be comfortable with the information provided by the simulation model, the ALCO members must understand the assumptions driving the model. Examples of some assumptions are:

- Demand deposits will grow by 20% during the next 12 months.
- The passbook rate will not be reduced unless the 90-day Treasury bill rate moves below 5.00%.
- Mortgage prepayment speed changes for various interest rate levels will be based on FNMA prepayment histories.
- The shape of the yield curve will remain constant for all interest rate scenarios.

The banking environment as well as the local and national economies are in a state of constant change. If the model is to provide an accurate simulation, the assumptions embedded in the model must be adjusted to reflect the real world. To accomplish this, the ALCO must review the primary model assumptions at least quarterly.

The latest development in the field of asset/liability management is the concept of the net value of portfolio equity. This is the net present value of the asset's cash flows less the net present value of the liability's cash flows. Most simulation models with the ability to calculate duration can compute the net value of the portfolio equity. These models use various interest rate scenarios to measure the change in the net value of portfolio equity for a given change in interest rates. The ALCO should review the effect of various rate scenarios on the net value of portfolio equity each quarter. If an interest rate change causes a significant decline in the net value of portfolio equity, the interest rate risk exposure could be too large and action may be warranted. The ALCO must decide how much of a decline in the net value of portfolio equity is unacceptable. Although one of the objectives of the ALCO is to maximize the net value of the institution, the committee must establish a minimum level for the net value of portfolio equity so they can, in a worst-case situation, preserve the value of the firm.

Capital is a critical element in the risk profile of any institution. An institution's capital acts as a cushion to absorb losses. The more capital a bank has, the more losses it is able to absorb. If an institution is thinly capitalized, a relatively minor loss can seriously deplete the capital position. Therefore, institutions must maintain at least a stated minimum capital position in order to operate. The institution must never allow its capital position to fall below the lowest limit established by the regulatory agencies. If the ALCO perceives an increase in the institution's credit risk or interest rate risk, the committee may decide to establish a minimum capital level in excess of the regulatory minimum. The larger capital base will enable the institution to absorb the losses that may occur as a result of the institution's higher risk profile. The ALCO must monitor the institution's capital position to be sure adequate capital levels are being maintained. To accomplish this task, most standard report packages include a core (leverage) and risk-based capital analysis as the detailed reports supporting the capital summary statement.

There is no one correct set of reports that must be used by the ALCO. However, the reports described in this chapter should provide an adequate information base for the ALCO meetings. As the ALCO members increase their knowledge and become more experienced in the asset/liability management process, and as new theories and technologies evolve, new reports will be added, reports will be deleted, and old report formats will be changed.

How frequently ALCO meetings should be scheduled is a matter of organizational structure and individual preference. Those ALCOs that delegate the daily pricing of loans and deposits to other committees within the organization may find that monthly meetings are adequate. However, ALCOs that directly price loans and deposits may meet weekly or even daily to adjust the products' pricing and meet once each month to discuss strategies and review the standard report package. Over time, each institution must adjust the frequency of the ALCO meetings until it discovers the meeting schedule that works best. What is essential for all

Table 2.1 ALCO's Agenda/Action Items Required to Establish the A/L Management Process

- Define the role of the ALCO within the organization
- Establish goals for the ALCO
- Decide how interest rate risk is to be measured
- Determine the parameters within which the level of interest rate risk is considered acceptable
- Decide what constitutes available liquidity
- Determine how much liquidity is required to operate the institution safely and effectively
- List the A/L management reports the ALCO will require
- Begin searching for a simulation model
- Establish a regular meeting time
- Appoint a secretary to take the minutes at the ALCO meeting
- Write the asset/liability management policy and submit it to the board of directors for their approval

ALCOs is to have regularly scheduled meetings and keep a set of minutes documenting the discussions and recording the decisions of the committee. Table 2.1 presents a summary of the issues that must be addressed at the first ALCO meetings.

3

Selecting and Implementing an Asset/Liability Model

electing an appropriate asset/liability model is an important part of the asset/liability management process. Since the late 1970s when the commercially available A/L models were first offered, substantial improvements have occurred in software and hardware products.

By reviewing the questions and issues raised in this chapter, and investigating the various features available in A/L models, managers can narrow the range of models they might want to consider for purchase. This process will provide the foundation for a preliminary comparison of models and enable A/L managers to raise the questions that are critical to determining which model will best meet an institution's requirements.

Models are varied and complex. No survey of manageable length could cover all the topics about which a potential buyer would want to know. The capabilities of the various models should be discussed directly with the vendor in conjunction with a review of available literature and a demonstration of the vendor's model. Figure 3.1 is a list of simulation model vendors with their mailing addresses and telephone numbers.

When making a selection, the buyer should consider the following:

- Will it be an effective tool?
- Are training, consultation and support important in the decision-making process?
- How many active users are there of the model under consideration?
- How many new clients have purchased each vendor's model within the past twelve months?

Mike Parentice	(617) 890-7730	Jerry W Weiner	(800) 879-1996
Banking Decisions Systems		Interactive Planning Systems	
950 Winter Street		330 Research Court, Suite 100	
Waltham 02154		Norcross, GA 30092	
Mel Strauss	(212) 432-8138	Penny Vasquez	(405) 842-1400
Chase Manhattan Bank		James Baker & Company	
1 World Trade Center, 78th Floor		1601 Northwest Expressway, Suite 2000	
New York, NY 10048		Oklahoma City, OK 73118	
Bob Goedken	(800) 356-9099	Leo Pylypec	(301) 982-0400
Profitstar		Olson Research Associates, Inc.	
11128 John Galt Blvd., Suite 350		10290 Old Columbia Road	
Omaha, NB 68137		Columbia, MD 21046	
Sharon Howard	(800) 321-6899	Kristy Gagstetter	(901) 762-5893
Sendero Corporation		Vining-Sparks	
7272 East Indian School Road, Suite 300		6077 Primacy Parkway, Suite 427	
Scottsdale, AZ 85251		Memphis, TN 38119	
Brian McNiff	(508) 794-0212	Liz Bergquist	(312) 683-2381
Warrington Financial Systems		Bank Administration Institute	
1 Corporate Drive		1 North Franklin Street	
Andover, MA 01801		Chicago, IL 60606	
Pat DeRubertis	(818) 992-4447	Deedee Myers	(602) 840-0606
DPSC Software		Myers - Kohl Corp.	
23501 Park Sorrento, Suite 105		4350 East Camel Back Rd., Suite 250 B	
Calabasas, CA 91302		Phoenix, AZ 85018	
Terry White	(913) 677-3383	Tom Charlton	(501) 220-5100
GRA, Thompson, White & Co.		Systematics Information Services, Inc.	
6740 Antioch Road, P.O. Box 29118		4001 Rodney Parham Road	
Shawnee Mission, KS 66201-1418		Little Rock, AR 72212-2496	
David Crandon	(213) 458-2604	Rob Cohen	(617) 848-5800
Treasury Services Corp.		BancWare, Inc.	
1222 Sixth Street		35 Braintree Hill Office Park, Suite 205	
Santa Monica, CA 90401		Braintree, MA 02184	

Figure 3.1 Simulation Model Vendors

- Are there frequent updates and new releases of the existing software product?
- Should the selection be based on the existing "process" in the organization, or should the selection of the model take into consideration possible changes in the process?
- Have you considered the level of staff sophistication,

both of the selected vendor, and of your in-house personnel?

- Are the necessary data and time available to prepare and present the informational output of the model?
- What is the vendor's philosophy of asset/liability management?
- What is the initial cost vs. the full cost of getting the system operational? (The amount of follow-up costs in terms of time and energy necessary to get the model functional and to maintaining it on an ongoing basis should be considered.)
- Have you checked an adequate number of references prior to purchase?
- Is the training performed at the client's location or at the vendor's office?
- What about ongoing support and education after the sale?
- Is the software compatible with existing equipment in the office/workplace, or will there be additional equipment purchases required?
- Have you evaluated the quality of training? (Be sure to discuss this item when referencing the vendor's client list.)
- What is the size of the vendor support staff and the financial strength of the vendor?
- Is the users' manual current and easy to use?

Shopping for a model can become quite complex. You can organize the process by constructing a model decision matrix

	Model X	Model Y	Model Z
VALUATION	YES	NO	YES
DURATION	YES	YES	YES
STATIC GAP REPORTS	YES	YES	YES
CASH FLOW	YES	YES	YES
WHAT IF SCENARIOS	YES	YES	YES
BASIS RISK	NO	NO	YES
G/L PROTOCOL	YES	YES	YES
DETAILED DATA LOADER	NO	NO	YES
FIVE YEAR PLANNING	NO	NO	YES
SYNTHETIC INSTRUMENTS	YES	YES	YES
USER-FRIENDLY	YES	YES	YES
PC BASED	YES	YES	YES
MAINFRAME BASED	NO	NO	NO
IBM COMPATIBLE	YES	YES	YES
HARDWARE PURCHASE	NO	NO	NO
GRAPHICS	NO	YES	YES
COST	$25,000	$75,000	$50,000

Figure 3.2 Model Decision Matrix

listing the prime considerations in the left column in conjunction with the models you are evaluating listed across the top row of the matrix (see Figure 3.2).

One of the important benefits of purchasing an A/L model is that they often provide useful financial tools that can aid in the preparation of the annual budget. They can provide a current year earnings simulation, or be used for strategic planning. While the A/L model should not be purchased solely for these capabilities, it is important to take these features into consideration.

First-time buyers of A/L software must not allow the model's features to dictate their approach to A/L management. This most often occurs with a basic model because it does not have the necessary flexibility. The ALCO must first determine its requirements, then begin the model search. Higher priced models tend to provide a higher degree of flexibility in meeting the ALCO's requirements.

Model Costs

The price of a simulation model can range between $3,000 and $90,000. An institution must not permit the price to deter it from purchasing the model that best meets its requirements. If the model helps the ALCO develop one successful action plan, it will have paid for itself many times over. The quoted price of most models includes only the software and the initial training. Many vendors also charge an annual fee for providing model improvements, user support, and an annual users' conference. The conference is a forum in which speakers present asset/liability management topics of current interest and demonstrate the newest features of the model.

DEVELOP A CHECKLIST OF CRITERIA AND PRIORITIZE EACH ITEM

In addition to the questions and issues mentioned earlier, it will be helpful to examine the following.

Information about the Company

Key issues such as financial stability, reputation, number of installations, and scope of service are some of the topics that should be raised when speaking with representatives of the vendor. It is important that the vendor stay in business, service and improve the model. Therefore, you must ask for the past two years' financial statements. Certain entrepreneurial and/or privately held corporations may be reluctant to offer this information; however, it is imperative that the ALCO members are certain the vendor is in sound financial condition.

Model Hardware Requirements

Most vendors are quite specific about the memory, disk space, and printer requirements necessary to run the system effectively. There may be ample capacity available on the institution's existing computer, in that case no hardware purchase will be necessary. However, most modeling systems will require the purchase of a personal computer system costing between $8,000 and $12,000.

Running speed is also an important criteria. Select a hardware configuration that will rapidly process the information and quickly print the reports. Slow systems can take over one hour to run a scenario while upgraded systems take only a few minutes.

Downloading Capability

Most models utilize direct input by the user of the financial data from the institution's general ledger. With this system, some accuracy is lost because average balances, average yields, and approximate maturities are frequently used as data inputs. If an institution has internal systems, or a service bureau that can download detailed information directly into the model, more reliable results can be obtained. Direct downloading also greatly simplifies the data input process and saves a great deal of the computer operator's time. This is an excellent option that can be found in only a few models.

Input Requirements

Many vendors have a standard set of input forms that must be carefully completed before the actual data input process can begin. This can be a difficult procedure for those not familiar with asset/liability models. The data input procedure will be accomplished much more quickly and accurately if the vendor will come on site to help load the data. This is a service that should be negotiated before the model is purchased.

User Manual and Help Screens

It is important for a model to have plenty of help screens in the program. When a question arises, or a new model operator is being trained, it is necessary to have clearly stated information presented to the operator in a well organized manner. Model buyers should carefully examine the help screens and users' manuals provided with each model to be sure they meet their requirements.

Index/Driver Rates

Most models permit the user to enter certain primary interest rates from which other rates used in the model are computed. When one of the primary or driver rates is changed, all the rates related to that rate will change. Models vary in the number of driver rates that can be used. When purchasing a model, it is important to be sure it has enough driver rates to meet the ALCO's requirements. For example, numerous driver rates are required to model the impact of changes in the shape of the yield curve on an institution's net interest margin.

Ability to Account for Synthetic Instruments (Futures, Swaps, Caps, etc.)

Synthetic instruments are now being utilized more frequently in the A/L process. Therefore, any model that does not offer this capability should not be considered for purchase. Even if an institution is not using synthetic instruments, there exists a high probability it will use them at some future date. When that situation occurs, it will be good to have a model that will accommodate the synthetic instruments.

It may be helpful to test the model before purchasing it with instruments currently being used by the institution. Because many instruments are written on a customized basis, with various interest rate indices, staggered maturities, and/or certain option limitations, the model being considered must have the ability to simulate their effect on the net interest income.

Historical Data

The ability to access historical data, such as balance sheets from past periods and changes in mortgage prepayment speeds during various stages of past business cycles, can be helpful when forecasting seasonal deposit fluctuations, cyclical loan demands, loan prepayment speeds and changes for various levels of interest rates. Only a few models offer this feature. Historical data storage is not essential for the successful operation of the models; however, it can enhance the accuracy of the model's projections.

Output/Reports

Reporting capabilities vary widely between the models. Most models produce dynamic balance sheet and income statements as well as a full set of static and dynamic gap reports. The reporting abilities of the models begin to diverge when such features as the ability to present the information in the form of a graph or a duration analysis report is requested.

Different modeling systems often present the same reports in very different ways. When shopping for a model, ask to see the actual reports generated by the model. It is important to have the information clearly presented in a format that is easy to read and understand. The model is the tool that generates the reports, but it is the reports that the ALCO will use as their primary tools for making decisions.

Model Installation Time

Once a selection has been made and the contract signed, it will typically take several weeks for the vendor and their training team to gather the necessary information and produce the first financial reports. During the installation of the model, senior management should be involved in the discussions of the characteristics of the financial institution's various products. Understanding how each asset and liability category interacts with a particular index/driver rate and the prepayment and/or growth levels associated with these categories is important to the overall accuracy of the model. Once the setup and first financial reports have been completed, the responsibility for operating the model can be delegated to others with senior management reviewing the assumptions and interpreting the results.

Vendor Support

As vendors strive to create more comprehensive, flexible, and accurate simulation models, the models become more complex. Even though there is an abundance of help screens embedded in the program and users' manuals are available, questions will arise during the modeling process that can be answered only by having access to the vendor's customer support staff. When evaluating the various models, talk with some of the support staff. They must have a thorough working knowledge of the model, be familiar with the asset/liability management process, and, most importantly, be willing to take the time to patiently work with a client to solve a problem or explain a feature of the model.

PLANNING THE IMPLEMENTATION

Once the model is selected, the planning phase of implementation begins. This phase is critical to the successful start of the A/L process. The process of installing and loading the data into the model will require A/L managers to spend a considerable amount of time working with the vendor's installation personnel. The process begins by developing a timeline for each component of the plan and determining the resources required to successfully complete the project. The implementation process may require one or two months. In-house support staff will be needed to develop a data gathering procedure and provide current data for the model. The number of support staff required depends on the size of the institution, the complexity of its general ledger, and the flexibility of loan and deposit reporting systems. The presence of vendor personnel on-site will greatly enhance the effectiveness of the institution's support staff in gathering data and formatting it in a fashion that is readily acceptable to the model.

The hardware will require several days to install and test. However, care and patience should be exercised because the system must be configured properly to speed the model's startup and run times. Most vendors are acquainted with the major hardware manufacturers and can assist with configuring the system.

CHART OF ACCOUNTS

The essence of most models is a defined chart of accounts. This chart may only remotely resemble the institution's actual chart of accounts because the interest rate sensitivity of each asset and liability type requires that a variable and a fixed component be identified and segregated. This is not an easy task, because the traditional trial balances for loans and deposits are rarely sorted by repricing characteristics. For many A/L managers, maturity data will be the only detailed information that is readily available. This does not usually represent a problem on the deposit side of the balance sheet. Most deposits have fixed rates and the trial balances contain maturity information by category. Recording the data by maturity enables the model to simulate cash flows and provides gap information. For floating rate deposits with a rate based on an index (i.e., Donahue Money Market), a single-line account can be established.

It is difficult to identify repricing rates for loans because each loan is unique. They use various rate indices, different margins, and a multitude of interest rate reset dates. However, for the model to function properly, it is necessary to separate each loan category into its fixed and variable components. For example:

One-to-four family—fixed rate mortgages

One-to-four family—adjustable rate mortgages (ARMs)

Commercial Real Estate—fixed rate

Commercial Real Estate—variable rate

Commercial & Industrial—fixed rate

Commercial & Industrial—variable rate

After the initial separation of fixed and variable rate loans, the loans are further categorized by interest rate sensitivity. The more categories used to represent the loan portfolio, the greater the model's accuracy.

It is not uncommon to discover that certain loan types cannot be separated into repricing buckets. Therefore, the A/L manager must develop meaningful data by approximating the repricing buckets. For example, a reasonable estimate of the amount of residential 1 year ARMs repricing each month is one twelfth of the total amount of the ARM portfolio. By inputing one twelfth of the portfolio into each month's data cell, the model will calculate results that are a reasonable estimate of the rate sensitivity of the loans. While this approach is somewhat imprecise, the results are not too unlike those obtained by using a detailed data download system.

Off balance sheet items (i.e., interest rate swaps, floors, caps, etc.) must be treated differently in the chart of accounts. If they are included as a normal balance sheet item, they will distort the balance sheet by inflating the amount of assets and liabilities. As a result, key financial ratios based on the total asset or total liability figures will become distorted (i.e., net income divided by total assets = ROA). Off balance sheet items do affect the interest rate risk position of an institution and must be taken into consideration. However, they must be excluded from the summary totals when producing the balance sheet.

If the data has been correctly entered into the model, the income and expense items will match those on the institution's published financial statements. For instance, the section of the chart of accounts dealing with noninterest income and noninterest expense items should mirror the actual income statement. An example of how the chart of accounts in a typical model might appear is as follows:

NONINTEREST INCOME

Account Number	Description
30xxxx	Trust Fees
31xxxx	Service Charges
32xxxx	Securities Gains (Losses)
33xxxx	Real Estate Servicing Fees
34xxxx	Miscellaneous Other Income
etc.	

NONINTEREST EXPENSES

Account Number	Description
40xxxx	Salaries and Wages
41xxxx	Fringe Benefits
42xxxx	Occupancy and Equipment
43xxxx	Professional Services
44xxxx	Marketing
etc.	

The amount in each category is obtained from the institution's general ledger in summary form and entered into the model. Each institution must determine whether the summary information provided by the model is adequate for its reporting purposes. If a greater degree of detail is required, the ALCO must direct the A/L manager to break apart the summary information and enter it using more specific data categories.

DOCUMENT PREPARATION AND THE
INPUT PROCESS

The development of input documents is the next phase of an A/L model implementation process. The structure of the documents provides a framework that will enable the institution to organize its' complex data. The previously identified chart of accounts serves as the means by which the data may be input into the model via direct data entry. The input documents provide the structure and discipline that assists the support staff in their data gathering. The institution can develop its own forms; however, most vendors will supply the necessary documents.

The A/L manager will find the FDIC call reports helpful in gathering the data. The call reports are prepared quarterly and are a good source of financial data. Unfortunately, there is very little focus on rate volatility. Schedule RC-J is the one section of the call report that provides information about the interest rate sensitivity and maturities of loans, deposits, and investment securities.

Gathering detailed data on loans and deposits is difficult. Breaking apart these categories by repricing dates and by maturity is a manual effort at many institutions. It is necessary to sort through trial balances, extract the information, and arrange it according to common elements. This process can be greatly facilitated by requesting your data center or service bureau to do a fine sort of the trial balances. The service bureau can then present the data in a report format consistent with the model's data categories. For example, a request can be made for each loan category to be sorted by:

- Interest rate
- Repricing date (if applicable)
- Maturity date
- Margin spread (i.e., ARMs = 2.50% over the relevant index)
- Index (i.e., prime rate, one-year Treasury note, LIBOR, etc.)
- Maximum life rate cap for ARMs
- Maximum annual rate adjustment cap for ARMs

Deposit information can be broken down into similar components. For example:

- Interest rate
- Repricing date (for variable rate deposits, if applicable)
- Maturity date

By selecting these or similar criteria, the A/L manager can organize the input data into meaningful groups with common characteristics. This will enable the model to provide greater accuracy when simulating the performance of the institution. If the user is unable to obtain the assistance of the data center in performing these data sorts, the only other alternative will involve a calculator, a lot of hard work, and patience.

Once the input documents have been prepared, the data are reconciled to a relevant set of financial statements. This effort will pay off by saving time after the model has been run and the output documents are analyzed for accuracy.

ASSUMPTIONS

Once the basic data is gathered, a determination of growth assumptions for both assets and liabilities must be made. Each category or item identified in the chart of accounts requires a factor of net growth (new business in excess of principal payments) or net reduction (principal payments in excess of new business). A/L managers must consult with division heads of the various lines of business within the organization to obtain their best estimate of the growth assumptions for assets or liabilities for which they are responsible. Most growth assumptions will be for a 12-month period, unless the organization is involved in longer-term strategic planning.

An example of a growth assumption for a loan type is as follows:

	Month 1	Month 12	Growth $	%
Comm. Real Estate	$xxx mill.	$xxx mill.	$xx mill.	x%

In this example, month 1 is the current input data. Month 12 is the resultant balance after the growth assumptions were added and the principal repayments subtracted. Many models will accept the growth assumptions only as the annual dollar growth, the account total in the final period, or as the annual percentage growth rate. In the advanced models, all of these methods are available to be used at the discretion of the user.

A review of the historical trend for each line item will serve as a reality check for the estimates provided by the division heads. If the trend in a particular deposit product has been a net growth in outstanding balances of 8% over the last 12 months, it is reasonable to assume the rate of growth for the next 12 months will be near the 8% level. If the division head estimates a growth rate significantly different from the last 12 months, the A/L manager must carefully review the projections to decide if the department head's growth assumptions should be used.

OPERATING THE MODEL

Processing time is dependent on the complexity of the model, the size of the chart of accounts, the number of data input entries, and the available memory and configuration of the computer. It is not uncommon to run the model frequently during the first weeks and months of a new installation. Repeated operation of the model is required to adjust output data delivered as part of the reporting process and to conduct trial runs as part of the initial debugging procedure.

The balance sheet is often used to verify the accuracy of the input process. It is commonplace to find discrepancies in several categories of assets and liabilities during the initial simulation run. Each variance must be researched and resolved, and the model run again to verify the changes. Once the model's balance sheet agrees with the institution's financial statements, it is helpful to turn to two other common system reports to verify the accuracy of the database.

The yield (or interest rate) report is most helpful in finding errors that result from the input process, or for building the chart of accounts. By scanning the various yields earned on assets, abnormalities can be discerned. Very often, a large variation indicates a potential problem. A review of the rates paid on the liabilities will indicate additional errors that must be corrected. A careful study of this report allows the A/L manager to correct input errors and establishes confidence in the interest rates used by the model to produce the income statement.

The income statement and the balance sheet are the primary reports management will use to test the credibility of the modeling process. If the A/L manager produces a series of reports for presentation to the ALCO, the balance sheet and income statement must agree with the institution's actual financial statements in order to develop confidence in the accuracy of the remaining reports.

STANDARDS AND INTERNAL DOCUMENTATION

An important aspect of model simulation is the development of internal standards and operating procedures. The need for an institution to identify the critical components of the total simulation process and operate the model in a consistent fashion that produces reliable reports is essential. The ever-present fact of employee turnover, coupled with continual product development, requires the A/L manager to develop and adhere to strict standards and procedures, such as the following:

- A standard chart of accounts must be maintained throughout the organization and involve all subsidiary companies.

- The input documents require standardization. Once established, these forms will streamline the entire process of data gathering and model input.
- Assumptions must be tested to be certain they are realistic and parallel actual performance.
- The model results should not simply be accepted as fact but should be challenged. This process will make sure the model reflects the ALCO members' best estimates and assumptions.

Internal documented procedures are critical to the modeling process. There is no single criticism that appears more frequently in audit reports than this issue. Documentation supplied by the vendor will, and should, be excellent. However, the internal work flow also must be documented. The A/L manager must answer such questions as:

- Who does the data input?
- From where does the detail data input originate?
- Are the data summarized in a fashion that fits the criteria of the model's requirements?
- How is the model output reconciled to published financials?
- Who provides the growth assumptions for the various lines of business?
- Does the model satisfy the requirements of the asset/liability management policy?

The ALCO must provide answers to these questions when implementing the modeling process. There is no one right set of answers, so each ALCO must base its answers on its institution's unique organizational structure and the individual abilities of its officers and staff.

SUMMARY

The selection of an asset/liability model is an important component of the management process. Its operation is designed to gather data and provide information that enables management to develop strategies that can significantly affect the institution's net interest income. The ALCO members must remember that the simulation model and the reports that are generated are not ends unto themselves. They are financial tools that, if carefully selected and skillfully maintained and operated, will reflect the ALCO members' best estimates of the institution's future performance.

4

Developing an Asset/Liability Management Policy

The asset/liability management policy serves two primary functions within the organization. First, the writing of the policy forces the ALCO to define the objectives and goals of the asset/liability management function and determine the degree of interest rate risk the institution is willing to tolerate. Second, the policy serves as the vehicle by which the board of directors can approve the institution's asset/liability management process and delegate authority for its implementation.

Most policies begin with a statement describing the general objectives of the asset/liability management function within the organization. Stating the objectives provides the basis for the asset/liability management policy. An example of a well-composed general statement is as follows:

> The asset/liability management function involves planning, directing, and controlling the flow, level, mix, cost, and yield of the consolidated funds of the corporation. These responsibilities are interwoven with the overall objectives of achieving the Corporation's financial goals and controlling the financial risks.

Following the opening statement the general goals are listed. These usually involve managing interest rate risk, increasing the institution's income, providing adequate liquidity, and preserving capital. The purpose of the general goals is to provide a broad focus as the framework for the more specific objectives to be defined later in the policy. Examples of some general goals are presented in the sample asset/liability management policy in the Appendix section at the end of this chapter. The sample policy illustrates the basic format and content of a standard asset/liability management policy.

The primary responsibility of the ALCO when writing the asset/liability management policy is to determine the institution's tolerance for accepting financial risks and articulate it when defining the risk parameters in the policy. Each financial institution is unique and this must be reflected in its policy. The policy must reflect the collective risk tolerance of senior managers and boards of directors which may vary from extremely conservative to very aggressive.

After the general objectives have been stated, a section describing the structure of the ALCO and its responsibilities is presented. This section designates the ALCO as being responsible for the institution's asset/liability process, describes the composition of the ALCO, mandates a regular meeting schedule, and requires the maintenance of minutes from each meeting. In this section, the requirement for an annual policy review and approval by the board of directors is stated and the responsibility for the selection, implementation, and monitoring of asset/liability management strategies is delegated to the ALCO.

INTEREST RATE RISK POLICY

The ALCO must determine the institution's risk tolerance and record it in the policy statement. To do this, the ALCO must decide which indicators to use as a measure of interest rate risks. The impact of a change in interest rates on a measure of income and the value of the institution are generally used as the indicators of interest rate risks. The net value of portfolio equity is used as a measure of the value of the institution and the net interest income, or the net income is frequently designated to measure income. The degree to which these indicators can decline for any given change in interest rates must be determined by the ALCO. For example, the ALCO may limit the net value of portfolio equity to no less than zero and restrict the level of net income to no less than zero. These limits assume that no institution wants to have a negative net worth or record a loss on their income statement.

Interest rate risk used to be defined in terms of the size of an institution's gap position. A plus or minus 10% one-year gap position was the standard interest rate risk limit. However, gap is no longer regarded as the best measure of interest rate risk and is not used as the primary measure in policy statements.

Since gap has ceased to be used as the principal measure of interest rate risks, there has been much confusion about what is the most effective measure. Regulatory agencies are now beginning to state their preferred approach to measuring the risks and are offering guidelines as to the magnitude of the rate shock tests to use when measuring interest rate risks. Since each regulatory body has a slightly different approach to defining interest rate risks, A/L managers should talk with the particular regulatory body with jurisdiction over their institution to find out their preferred approach to measuring interest rate risks before writing this section of the policy.

The impact of basis risk, prepayment risk, gap, and yield curve risk on an institution's income and value must be measured. By simulating the combined effect of balance sheet and off balance sheet items, the ALCO can measure the impact on the net interest income and the net value of portfolio equity for a given change in interest rates. The simulation model must be used to measure the total risk exposure of the institution because analyzing each type of interest rate risk in isolation would create a distorted image of the institution's exposure.

The policy must identify the limits within which the net interest income will be allowed to modulate. Many institutions define the limit in terms of a percentage variation in net interest income. For example, minus 20% might be considered the maximum tolerance for a decline in the net interest income during any 12-month period and a minus 10% decline could be established as the limit for longer time horizons. Another way to state the limits is to use the dollar variation method. The policy may state that the net interest income must not be permitted to decline more than XX million dollars during any 12-month period.

In determining the magnitude of interest rate changes to be used in the simulation model, some institutions use a constant change such as up 300 basis points and down 300 basis points. Others will adjust the magnitude of the up and down movement to reflect the prevailing level of interest rates. If short-term rates are 4%, the test might be down 100 basis points and up 300 basis points. However, if short-term rates are 8%, the test could be up and down 300 basis points.

The ALCO must account for all types of interest rate risk when using the simulation model to measure the institution's interest rate risk exposure. The simulation must reflect changes in the basis relationship between the various interest rates affecting the income statement, the effect of embedded options such as changes in the loan prepayment speeds, and changes in the shape of the yield curve. Some institutions include, as part of their policy, a statement that the simulation must include realistic assumptions about the effect of embedded options, changes in the basis relationships between rates, and variations in the shape of the yield curve.

INVESTMENT POLICY

Many institutions include a section in their asset/liability management policy that addresses how investments are used in the asset/liability management process. In some institutions, this has developed to the point where the investment policy is part of the asset/liability management policy.

The intent of the investment policy is to provide basic guidelines within which the investment portfolio can be managed to produce a superior return while providing an adequate source of liquidity and credit quality in the portfolio. Therefore, it is an integral part of the asset/liability policy. The investment policy should include the following objectives:

- Employ the funds of the Bank fully and efficiently when not needed to fund loan demand.
- Provide enough liquidity to meet potential withdrawals or increased loan demand.
- Maintain a maturity structure that is consistent with the bank's risk parameters.
- Provide adequate diversification between issuers, industries, and security types.
- Meet all regulatory and industry standards.
- Maintain a level of quality in the portfolio that will balance the credit risks of other assets.
- Seek maximum income within reasonable limits of risk consistent with liquidity and quality objectives.
- Take advantage of potentially attractive long-term total returns, where appropriate.

The ultimate responsibility for managing the investment portfolio resides with the board of directors who may delegate the authority to the senior investment officer. The policy must clearly indicate the delegation of responsibility. The investment policy must also limit the exposure to credit risk by restricting the amount that can be placed with any one issuer and requiring all securities to have an investment grade credit quality rating.

If the institution has designated a portion of its investment portfolio as a trading portfolio, it must be addressed in the investment policy. All securities held in a trading portfolio must be marked to market. This accounting requirement and the natural market risk of trading securities can create a high level of risk in the trading portfolio. Therefore, the investment policy must include an authorization from the board of directors to establish a trading account and define the maximum amount of securities held in the account.

CAPITAL POLICY

The policy must address the ALCO's responsibility for managing the institution's capital position. In most asset/liability policies, this consists of a brief passage stating that the ALCO is responsible for managing the institution's capital position and at no time will it be permitted to decline below the regulatory minimums. If the ALCO wants to establish a minimum capital position in excess of the regulatory limits, it should include a description of its minimum capital position limits in the policy.

The Financial Institutions Reform, Recovery, and Enforcement Act (FIRREA) of 1989 established new criteria for minimum capital requirements. The regulations introduced the concept of "risk-based" capital requirements. At the present time, risk-based capital takes only credit risk into consideration. The larger the amount of assets containing credit risk, the more capital is required to support them. Where high-risk (highly leveraged transactions, off balance sheet activities, etc.) transactions were once common in the 1980s, the capital requirements of the 1990s has reduced these activities by forcing management to evaluate the return against the exposed capital. The risk-based capital requirements combined with credit losses has left capital in short supply at many institutions.

An effective policy will address the need to meet minimum capital requirements and to operate a "safe and sound" institution. In so doing, the board of directors and the senior management must balance their responsibility to the shareholders to maximize the leverage of the capital with their fiduciary responsibility to protect the depositors. The numerous failures of financial institutions and the escalating liability claims against directors and officers have tempered the desire of many institutions to increase leverage. In developing a policy, the ALCO must balance the desires of management to maximize returns against the regulatory environment that encourages maximum Tier 1 capital.

The policy should also express any limits on the composition of the capital account. For example, the policy can restrict the amount of debt outstanding as a percent of capital or prohibit the use of preferred stock.

The board must have as its primary concern the preservation of capital. This is balanced against their responsibilities as elected individuals who serve the best interests of the shareholders by maximizing the value of the firm, improving the ROA, and more specifically the ROE.

The board has the fiduciary responsibility to ensure that a dividend policy is developed that is prudent and flexible given the financial performance of the institution. The policy must provide a dividend to enhance shareholder value, yet recognize restraint during periods when capital is impaired by negative earnings. The operation of a "safe and sound" institution is the fundamental objective of regulatory supervision. The capital markets recognize this philosophy, and will, in the long run, reward the appropriate use of capital.

LIQUIDITY POLICY

In addition to being responsible for managing the institution's interest rate risk and capital position, the ALCO is responsible for managing its liquidity position. The next section of the asset/liability statement should designate the ALCO as being responsible for managing the institution's liquidity position. If special facilities are required, such as using brokered deposits, purchasing federal funds, or using reverse repurchase agreements for short-term borrowing purposes, the approval should be stated here and any dollar limits or other restrictions described.

During an examination by any of the regulatory bodies the examiners will read the asset/liability management policy. They want to make sure management is complying with the policy and that the policy defines an asset/liability management process that is adequate to successfully manage the institution's interest rate risks, liquidity needs, and capital position. Since each regulatory agency has different criteria for evaluating an asset/liability management policy, the A/L manager should contact their governing regulatory agency to learn its criteria prior to drafting the policy.

When developing the components of a liquidity policy, the following issues are appropriate for inclusion:

General Policy Statements

■ This section will be broad-based and deal with a variety of issues, such as: the ability of the institution to maintain adequate liquidity; the avoidance of undue risk; the frequency that liquidity will be monitored; addressing the regulatory requirements; a statement of policy limitations for ratios to be used to measure liquidity; and the establishment of guidelines to manage the mix of funding composition to enhance liquidity.

Statement Objectives

■ The purpose of this segment of the policy will be to provide liquidity guidelines for meeting deposit outflows, new loan growth, payment of taxes, and other anticipated cash needs. Ideally, liquidity levels will be higher at times of rising rates and lower at times of declining rates.

Delineation of Authority to Measure and Manage Liquidity

■ This section delegates the authority and the responsibility for managing the institution's liquidity position. It identifies entities such as the board of directors and the ALCO as being responsible for managing the institution's liquidity position. It should also discuss limits and conditions under which these authorities may pass responsibility to the next layer of management.

Responsibility for Compliance

■ This section should address which governing body (i.e., board of directors, ALCO) or individual is charged with the responsibility for compliance of policy issues. In most cases, it will be the ALCO's responsibility, reporting directly to the board of directors.

Ratio Definitions and Limits

■ This section addresses the liquidity parameters that the ALCO will monitor. The regulatory authorities use:
  a. Dependency Ratio
  b. Liquidity Ratio
  c. Brokered Deposits divided by Total Deposits
  d. Net Loans and Leases divided by Total Assets
■ The worksheet provided in (Figure 4.1) will assist the ALCO in preparing the factors used in the ratios. Once completed, the ratios can then be determined.

Certain assets can be used to obtain short term funds through reverse repurchase agreements or can be used to secure longer term borrowings. These assets should be available to provide collateral for funding liquidity to the institution. Therefore, they should not be pledged unless absolutely necessary. Assets which can not be used for collateral in their present form, such as automobile or credit card loans, can be transformed into acceptable collateral by converting them into a marketable security. The liquidity policy can state that management will keep an adequate amount of collateral available for liquidity borrowing needs at all times and make provisions for securitizing loans if necessary to meet the requirement.

The policy should address contingencies for providing additional collateral requirements in difficult financial times. Typically, rating agencies will begin to lower debt ratings during these times. Due to the fact that corporate customers and consumers are placing greater emphasis on ratings provided by credit agencies, they will react quickly when news events or an announced decline in ratings occurs. An internal and external communications vehicle must be established as a component of the policy. Should a liquidity crisis ever occur, immediate and effective communication between the management of the institution, the Federal Reserve Bank and the public press will aid the liquidity management process.

SUMMARY

During an examination by any of the regulatory agencies, the field examiners will review the asset/liability management policy. They want to make sure management, under the auspices of the board of directors, is complying with the

LIQUIDITY RATIO AND DEPENDENCY RATIO

Amounts Are From FDIC Call Report Schedules	AMOUNT ($ millions)	TOTALS
SHORT TERM INVESTMENTS (Due in One Year or Less)		
1. Temporary Investments (Per UBPR Definition)	53,562	
2. Adjustments: Other Money Market Instruments (Describe)		
3. TOTAL SHORT TERM INVESTMENTS		$ 53,562
OTHER MARKETABLE ASSETS (Due Over One Year)		
4. U.S. and Agency Securities (BV)	114,659	
5. Other Investment Quality Securities (BV)	28,663	
6. Other Marketable Assets—Real Estate Mortgages Available for Resale	9,909	
—Equity Securities	241	
—Sub-investment Debt Securities	225	
7. TOTAL OTHER MARKETABLE ASSETS		153,697
ADD:		
8. Cash and Noninterest-bearing Depository Balances	27,241	
9. Appreciation In Above Securities	1,532	
9.a. Subtotal	28,773	
LESS:		
10. Reserve Requirements Being Met By Any Of Above	13,907	
11. Liabilities Secured By Any Of Above	4,997	
12. Depreciation In Above Securities	0	
12.a. Subtotal............	18,904	
13. NET CASH, SHORT TERM, AND MARKETABLE ASSETS		217,128

68

	Percent (%)	AMOUNT ($ millions)	TOTALS
14. Total Brokered Deposits		0	
15. Other Time Deposits $100M And Over	3	29,529	
16. Deposits Held In Foreign Offices...............		0	
17. Fed Funds Purchased And Repos		888	
18. Other Borrowings And Debt Due In One Year ...	1	3,846	
19. Adjustments: (Describe)	0	0	
20. TOTAL POTENTIALLY VOLATILE LIABILITIES (ADJUSTED)	4		$ 34,263
OTHER DEPOSITS			
21. All Other Deposits Not Listed Above	96	911,250	
22. Adjustments: (Describe)	0	0	
23. TOTAL OTHER DEPOSITS (Adjusted)			911,250
24. TOTAL DEPOSITS AND SHORT TERM LIABILITIES	100%		945,513
25. LESS: Item 11 Above			4,997
26. NET DEPOSITS AND SHORT TERM LIABILITIES			$940,516
* * LIQUIDITY RATIO—Line 13 Divided By Line 26 * * *			23.09%

LONG TERM ASSETS FUNDED WITH POTENTIALLY VOLATILE LIABILITIES (Adjusted)

27. Net Potentially Volatile Liabilities (Assets) Line 20 Minus Line 3			(19,299)
28. Total Earning Assets Minus Line 3			897,473
* * DEPENDENCY RATIO—Line 27 Divided By Line 28 * * *			(2.15)%

Source: Federal Deposit Insurance Corporation

Figure 4.1 Liquidity and Dependency Ratio Analysis

policy. Also, they want to be assured that the policy defines an asset/liability management process that is adequate to successfully manage the institution's interest rate risks, liquidity needs, and capital position. Since each regulatory agency has different criteria for evaluating an asset/liability management policy, a member of the ALCO should talk with their governing agency to learn their criteria prior to drafting the policy.

APPENDIX: A BASIC ASSET/LIABILITY MANAGEMENT POLICY

The asset/liability management function involves planning, directing, and controlling the flow, level, mix, cost, and yield of the consolidated funds of the Corporation. These responsibilities are interwoven with the overall objectives of achieving the Corporation's financial goals and controlling financial risks.

General Goals

1. Keep the level of interest rate risk within the stated limits.
2. Enhance the Corporation's net interest income.
3. Provide adequate liquidity.
4. Maintain adequate capital.

The Asset/Liability Management Committee

Responsibility for the implementation of the asset/liability management process resides with the asset/liability management committee (ALCO). The committee is co-chaired by the Corporation's treasurer and chief investment officer. Other members of the committee include the chairman, president, executive vice president in charge of banking operations, executive vice president in charge of lending, and any additional members as may be deemed appropriate by the committee. The committee meets on a monthly basis to review the components of the Corporation's overall ALCO policy as described herein. Minutes are taken at each meeting and retained for future reference.

The board of directors reviews the asset/liability management policy on an annual basis and delegates responsibility for the selection, implementation, and monitoring of the various strategies required to meet the ALCO policy objectives to the A/L management committee and those individuals whom the committee deems appropriate to execute such transactions.

Net Interest Income Analysis

The corporation will maintain an interest rate risk position such that the financial shock of a 300 basis point increase or a 300 basis point decrease in the current rate structure will not cause a decline in the net interest income in excess of XXXX million dollars. Also, in the worst-case scenario, the net interest income must be sufficient to cover the bank's net operating expenses exclusive of extraordinary provisions to the loan loss reserve and security gains/losses. The minimum acceptable amount of net value of portfolio equity that must be maintained at all times is four percent of total assets. The model used to produce the simulation analysis must employ realistic basis risks, prepayment speeds and yield curve slope change assumptions.

The asset/liability management committee is responsible for maintaining the Bank's net interest income. To accomplish this, the committee establishes the general guidelines for the pricing strategies for loans and deposits. The implementation of the strategies is delegated to the deposit pricing committee and the loan committee.

In order to maintain the net interest margin within the risk parameters as defined above, the Bank will occasionally enter into interest rate swap, floor, and cap agreements. The other party to the agreements must be a major commercial bank acting as principal and be rated B or better by the Thomson BankWatch Service. The limit on the net amount of swaps, caps, or floors employed will be determined by the net interest income variation parameters defined above. These agreements will be entered into only as a hedge to the Bank's interest rate risk exposure. Authorization to enter such transactions will be granted by the ALCO, and will be executed by a designated member of the committee.

Liquidity Management

The asset/liability management committee is responsible for monitoring and maintaining an adequate level of liquidity such that the Corporation will have funds available to meet cash commitments at all times, at a reasonable cost. Among the financial tools the committee can use to provide liquidity are the various Federal Funds borrowing facilities, brokered CD relationships (brokered CDs may not exceed XX% of total deposits), and reverse repurchase agreement facilities using unpledged Treasury securities, agency securities and securitized mortgages.

Capital

The capital position of the corporation will at no time be less than the required regulatory minimums. Management will strive to maintain a capital position necessary to the corporation's long-term financial health through earnings performance and the ability to issue Tier 2 subordinated debt.

5

Identifying and Measuring the Risks

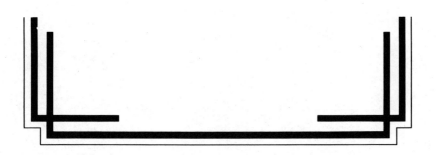

Banking, when reduced to its basic essence, is simply a financial arbitrage. Money is obtained by paying a certain rate of interest and is redeployed at a higher interest rate. If the difference between the two rates (net interest margin) is more than sufficient to cover the various expenses associated with operating the financial institution, a profit is produced. This chapter will discuss the risks inherent in this arbitrage.

IDENTIFYING THE RISKS

Credit Risk

Credit risk arises with the possibility that a bank will not receive the principal and/or interest due on a loan or investment. This risk becomes more evident when the economy enters a period of recession. A decline in sales reduces corporate revenues, making it difficult for some corporations to service their debt obligations. As a result, many financially weak businesses and corporations will be unable to pay the interest and/or principal due on their loans. When this occurs, it will often produce a financial loss for the lender. Although this is one of the primary risks encountered in banking, the management of credit risk usually lies beyond the responsibility of the asset/liability management committee. Most banks delegate the management of credit risk to the lending and investment areas of the bank.

The greatest credit risk occurs in the bank's lending function. Since many of the loans a bank makes are to individuals, local corporations, and privately owned businesses, their creditworthiness is often not reviewed or rated by nationally recognized credit assessment firms, such as Moody's and Standard and Poor's. For this reason, the evaluation of the corporate borrowers' ability to repay is left to the discretion of each bank's credit department and its lending officers. At many banks, the credit risk is controlled by a loan review or credit committee, comprised of experienced lending officers, that reviews large loans before approval is granted.

Loans are generally a bank's highest yielding asset. During the period 1985–1990, the average prime lending rate was 9.35%, while the average yield available on a 90-day Treasury bill was 7.01%. The extra 2.34% of interest income produced by the loan is the risk premium received by the bank for incurring the additional risk. A bank with a low loan-to-deposit ratio (total loans divided by total deposits) can improve its earnings by shifting more of its assets into loans. On the other hand, if the growth of the loan portfolio is achieved by relaxing the bank's credit standards, higher loan losses may offset the income generated by the additional loans. To produce the maximum amount of profits, it is essential for a bank to carefully manage its exposure to credit risk in the loan portfolio.

Managing the credit risk that occurs in the investment portfolio is a much simpler process than managing the credit risk in the loan portfolio. Except for junk bonds and nonrated issues, most of the fixed income investments are debt issues of the federal government, its agencies, municipal entities, and major corporations. Because U.S. Treasury bills, notes, and bonds are federal government debt instruments, they are considered to be free from credit risk. The same is generally true of federal agency debt instruments. The larger corporations and municipal entities are analyzed and rated by Moody's and Standard and Poor's and are closely followed by other Wall Street analysts.

If problems develop at one of the major corporations or municipal entities, impairing its creditworthiness, reports in the financial press will bring it to the attention of the bank's portfolio manager. The manager will also be made aware of the deteriorating credit situation when the national rating agencies lower the rating on the outstanding debt instruments. Most credit risk in the investment portfolio is managed by an investment policy committee. The committee limits the bank's exposure to credit risk by establishing an investment policy that generally restricts the bank's investments to direct obligations of the U.S. government, its agencies, political subdivisions, and major corporations. These securities must have a credit rating that meets the minimum credit quality standards set by the committee. If the credit risk in the bank's balance sheet is being adequately managed by the lending division and the investment policy committee, the remaining risks will all involve changes in interest rates and liquidity requirements.

Interest Rate Risk

Until a few years ago, the most fundamental measure of interest rate risk was the gap position. Gap is the difference between the amount of assets and liabilities on which the interest rates are reset during any given time period. For example, if a bank has only one, $1 million, 90-day term deposit paying 8%; and invests the $1 million in a 90-day fixed-rate loan earning 10% and maturing on the same day as the deposit, the bank will have a matched gap. As defined by gap, there would be no interest rate risk. If interest rates rise 100 basis points during the 90-day term of the deposit, the deposit will be renewed at 9% and the fixed-rate loan will also mature and be renewed at 11%. Thus, the 2% net interest margin will be preserved (Table 5.1).

If the proceeds of the 90-day term deposit are invested in a floating-rate loan with an initial rate of 10%, the interest earned on the loan will change throughout the 90-day period while the deposit rate remains unchanged. Since the asset is repricing much more rapidly than the liability during this period, the bank is asset sensitive. The asset-sensitive bank will produce a larger net interest margin if rates rise because the interest rate earned on the loan, which initially was 10%, will move higher during the 90-day period, while the interest rate being paid on the deposit remains at 8% (Table 5.2). Conversely, the asset-sensitive gap position will cause a compression in the net interest margin as interest rates decline. The loan initially earning 10% will earn less as interest rates decline while the cost of the deposit remains at 8% (Table 5.3).

If the bank uses the proceeds of the $1 million, 8%, 90-day term deposit to make a $1 million, 30-year fixed-rate mort-

Table 5.1 Matched Gap Position

	Yield/Cost Before Rate Change	Yield/Cost At Reset Date	
		Rates Rising	Rates Declining
90-Day Fixed Rate Loan	10.00%	11.00%	9.00%
90-Day Term Deposit	8.00%	9.00%	7.00%
Net Interest Margin	2.00%	2.00%	2.00%

Table 5.2 Asset-Sensitive Position with Rising Rates

	Yield/Cost Before Rate Change	Yield/Cost After 30 Days	Yield/Cost After 60 Days
Floating Rate Loan	10.00%	11.00%	12.00%
90-Day Term Deposit	8.00%	8.00%	8.00%
Net Interest Margin	2.00%	3.00%	4.00%

gage at 10%, the mortgage will continue to earn 10% while the deposit reprices every 90 days. The bank is now liability sensitive because the rate paid on its deposit is reset more rapidly than the rate being received on the loan. A rise or fall in interest rates in a liability-sensitive bank has the opposite effect on the net interest margin than a bank that is asset sensitive. If interest rates decline, the mortgage will continue to earn 10% during the next 30 years, and at each 90-day maturity date, the term deposit will be renewed at a lower rate than the initial 8% rate (Table 5.4).

An increase in interest rates will cause an erosion of the liability-sensitive bank's net interest margin. The mortgage

Table 5.3 Asset-Sensitive Position with Declining Rates

	Yield/Cost Before Rate Change	Yield/Cost After 30 Days	Yield/Cost After 60 Days
Floating Rate Loan	10.00%	9.00%	8.00%
90-Day Term Deposit	8.00%	8.00%	8.00%
Net Interest Margin	2.00%	1.00%	–0–

Table 5.4 Liability-Sensitive Position with Declining Rates

	Yield/Cost Before Rate Change	Yield/Cost After First Reset Date	Yield/Cost After Second Reset Date
30-Year Fixed Rate Mortgage	10.00%	10.00%	10.00%
90-Day Term Deposit	8.00%	7.00%	6.00%
Net Interest Margin	2.00%	3.00%	4.00%

will continue to earn 10% over the next 30 years, but at each 90-day maturity date of the term deposit it will be renewed at a higher rate than the initial 8% rate. If the prevailing 90-day deposit rate increases to the point where it exceeds the 10% rate being earned on the mortgage loan, a negative net interest margin will be produced (Table 5.5).

This is precisely what happened in the late 1970s and early 1980s, when soaring interest rates and the deregulation of financial institutions combined to cause many savings and loans and savings banks to generate losses. For decades

Table 5.5 Liability-Sensitive Position with Rising Rates

	Yield/Cost Before Rate Change	Yield/Cost After First Reset Date	Yield/Cost After Second Reset Date
30-Year Fixed Rate Mortgage	10.00%	10.00%	10.00%
90-Day Term Deposit	8.00%	9.00%	10.00%
Net Interest Margin	2.00%	1.00%	–0–

under the protection of government regulation, the banks used low-cost, short-term deposits to fund 30-year fixed-rate mortgages. As the banking industry became deregulated, interest rates moved higher, and financial institutions paid sharply higher rates of interest when maturing short-term deposits were renewed.

The tremendous losses generated at many liability-sensitive institutions between 1978 and 1983 made bankers painfully aware of the risk of a mismatched gap position. The impact of that experience caused the federal and state regulators to require banks to periodically measure their interest rate risk position and put in place interest rate risk management policies that limit the amount of interest rate risk assumed by the institution. Mismatched repricing periods of assets and liabilities is only one form of interest rate risk. There are other forms of interest rate risk inherent in every bank's balance sheet that can severely impact a bank's earnings.

Basis Risk

To identify the other types of interest rate risks, it is useful to return to the previous example of the bank's perfectly matched gap position. As defined by gap, the bank had no interest rate risk in its balance sheet because the interest rate paid on the 90-day deposit and the interest rate earned on the 90-day fixed rate loan reset on exactly the same day. Although it is clear that there is no timing difference between the reset dates, it is not clear that the magnitude of the change in the deposit rate will be exactly matched by the magnitude of the change in the loan rate. A review of the history of interest rate movements indicates that the interest rates on two different instruments will seldom change by the same amount during the same period of time.

In the example of a bank with a matched gap position, the 90-day deposit rate changed from 8% to 9% as the rate being earned on the 90-day fixed-rate loan changed from 10% to 11%, thus preserving the 2% net interest margin. In reality, if the change in the deposit rate increases from 8% to 9%, the rate being earned on the loan will usually increase by more than 100 basis points. The current risk premium in the lending rate used in this example is 25% of the 90-day term deposit rate (8.00% × 1.25 = 10.00%). If the risk premium remains constant, as the 90-day term deposit rate moves from 8.00% to 9.00%, the rate being earned on the loan will move from 10.00% to 11.25% (9.00% × 1.25 = 11.25%). This will produce a 25 basis point increase in the net interest margin from 2% to 2.25% (Table 5.6 Example 1). If after operating expenses this bank is producing a pretax return on assets (ROA) of 100 basis points, the 25 basis point expansion in the net interest margin will increase the ROA to 125 basis points. This creates a 25% increase in ROA. In this example, the unequal magnitude of the change in the two interest rates work to the bank's advantage by increasing the ROA 25%.

Table 5.6 Basis Risk Illustration

	Yield/Cost Before Rate Change	Yield/Cost Example 1	Yield/Cost Example 2
90-Day Fixed Rate Loan	10.00%	11.25%	10.75%
90-Day Term Deposit	8.00%	9.00%	9.00%
Net Interest Margin	2.00%	2.25%	1.75%

Risk premiums change over time as the perception of risk changes in the market place. If the 25% risk premium used in the previous example shrinks to 19.4%, the 100 basis point increase in the rate being paid on the deposit produces only a 75 basis point increase in the rate being earned on the loan ($9.00\% \times 1.194 = 10.75$), the net interest margin contracts by 25 basis points (Table 5.6 Example 2) and the bank's ROA declines from 100 basis points to 75 basis points. The fact that the bank's gap remains perfectly matched while changes in the level of interest rates cause wide swings in the bank's profits, clearly indicates another form of interest rate risk is present and illustrates the problem of using gap as the primary measure of an institution's interest rate risk.

The risk to a bank's profitability exists when a change in the general level of interest rates causes the rates on various types of instruments to change with different magnitudes and is referred to as basis risk. When the variation in the degree by which the rates move causes the net interest margin to expand, the bank has experienced a favorable basis shift. On the other hand, if the variation in the rate movements causes the net interest margin to contract, the basis has moved against the bank.

The basis risk inherent in every bank's balance sheet is as individual as a fingerprint. For this reason, each bank's asset/liability management committee must be well aware of the basis risk inherent in their institution's balance sheet. Deposit rates in various regions of the country and in different cities and towns will change by different amounts during the same time period. Also, variations in the composition of banks' asset structures will cause each bank's earning asset rate to change by a different amount for any given change in the general level of interest rates. The various

Table 5.7 Basis Risk Analysis: Prime Lending Rate Minus Federal Funds Rate: 3/31/85–3/30/90*

Average Spread	1.73%
Standard Deviation	0.31
Variance	0.09
Widest Spread	3.06%
Narrowest Spread	0.25%

*(Illustrated on Figure 5.1)

methods of identifying and measuring a bank's basis risk is further discussed in greater detail in Chapters 6 and 7.

Examples of the amount of basis risk that can occur are illustrated in Tables 5.7 and 5.8 as well as in Figures 5.1 and 5.2. In these examples, rates on instruments of identical maturities are compared. The amount of variation in the spread between these rates provides actual illustrations of the significant impact that basis risk can have on a bank's net interest margin.

Net Interest Position Risk

A bank's net interest position also exposes the bank to additional interest rate risk and can be considered as another

Table 5.8 Basis Risk Analysis: One-Year CD Rates Minus One-Year Treasury Bill Rates: 3/31/85–3/30/90*

Average Spread	0.47%
Standard Deviation	0.47
Variance	0.22
Widest Spread	1.67%
Narrowest Spread	−1.11%

*(Illustrated on Figure 5.2)

form of basis risk. If a bank has more assets on which it earns interest than it has liabilities on which it pays interest, the bank is said to have a positive net interest position. In other words, the bank will have earning assets being funded by noncosting liabilities. A bank with a large positive net interest position is very fortunate because it funds a large amount of interest-earning assets with liabilities on which it pays no interest. The risk arises from the net interest position when the interest rates earned on the assets change while the cost of the funding liabilities remains unchanged at zero percent (Table 5.9). Thus, a bank with a positive net interest position will experience a reduction in its net interest margin as interest rates decline and an expansion in its net interest margin as rates rise.

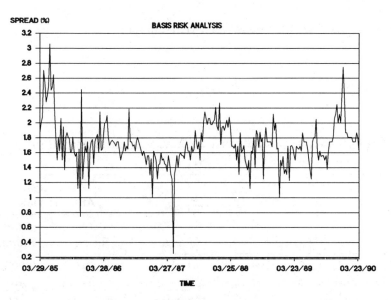

Figure 5.1 Prime rate minus federal fund rate

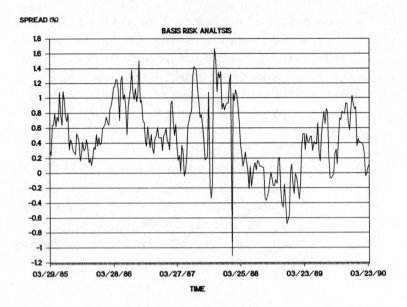

Figure 5.2 1 yr. CD rate minus 1 yr. T-bill rate

Table 5.9 Effect of Interest Rate Movements on a Bank's Positive Net Interest Position

	Yield/Cost Before Rate Change	Yield/Cost At Reset Date	
		Rates Rising	Rates Falling
90-Day Fixed Rate Loan	10.00%	11.00%	9.00%
Demand Deposit	–0–	–0–	–0–
Net Interest Margin	10.00%	11.00%	9.00%

Large positive net interest positions account for most of the profits generated at many financial institutions. Although a large positive net interest position is certainly desirable, the variation in earnings that it causes as interest rates move may not be desirable. Chapter 6 will discuss various strategies to reduce the variation in profits that can be created by the net interest position.

Embedded Option Risks

Large changes in the general level of interest rates create another source of risk to a bank's profits by encouraging the prepayment of loans and bonds and/or the withdrawal of term deposits before their stated maturity dates. In the example of the matched gap position illustrated in Table 5.1, it is assumed that the 90-day fixed-rate loan and the 90-day term deposit are in place until their maturity date. In actuality, that is not what happens. If there are no substantial penalties for prepaying the loan, the borrower will come to the bank after a decline in rates occurs and pay off his 10% loan with a new loan at 9%. If this occurs 30 days after the original loan is made, the bank will receive the 200 basis point net interest margin for only 30 days rather than the anticipated 90 days. In the remaining 60 days of the 90-day term, the net interest margin will be only 100 basis points (Table 5.10). The bank had anticipated earning 200 basis points in the 90-day period; instead it earned an average net interest margin of 133 basis points. That is a 33% drop in the net interest margin due entirely to the prepayment of the loan.

When rates rise the net interest margin becomes exposed to the same embedded option risk, except that it now occurs

Table 5.10 Embedded Option Risk with Declining Rates

	Yield/Cost First 30 Days	Yield/Cost Second 30 Days	Yield/Cost Third 30 Days
With No Loan Prepayment			
90-Day Fixed-Rate Loan	10.00%	10.00%	10.00%
90-Day Term Deposit	8.00%	8.00%	8.00%
Net Interest Margin	2.00%	2.00%	2.00%
With Loan Prepayment			
90-Day Fixed-Rate Loan	10.00%	9.00%	9.00%
90-Day Term Deposit	8.00%	8.00%	8.00%
Net Interest Margin	2.00%	1.00%	1.00%

on the liability side of the balance sheet. If there are no substantial penalties for early withdrawal, the depositor will withdraw the term deposit before maturity so the funds can be redeposited in a new 90-day term deposit account at a higher rate. For example, if a 100 basis point rise in rates occurs 30 days after the deposit is made, the depositor would close out his 8%, 90-day term account and open a new 90-day term account paying 9%. This action will cause the bank's net interest margin to decline to 100 basis points during the last 60 days of the original 90-day term (Table 5.11). The average net interest margin for the 90-day period will be 133 basis points rather than the originally anticipated 200 basis point net interest margin.

As interest rates rise and fall, all banks are exposed to some degree of risk as the customers exercise the embedded options inherent in their loans and deposits. The faster the

Table 5.11 Embedded Option Risk with Rising Rates

	Yield/Cost First 30 Days	Yield/Cost Second 30 Days	Yield/Cost Third 30 Days
With No Early Deposit Withdrawal			
90-Day Fixed-Rate Loan	10.00%	10.00%	10.00%
90-Day Term Deposit	8.00%	8.00%	8.00%
Net Interest Margin	2.00%	2.00%	2.00%
With Early Deposit Withdrawal			
90-Day Fixed-Rate Loan	10.00%	10.00%	10.00%
90-Day Term Deposit	8.00%	9.00%	9.00%
Net Interest Margin	2.00%	1.00%	1.00%

change in rates and the greater the magnitude of the change, the greater will be the embedded option risk to the bank's net interest margin. Most banks protect themselves from the risk by imposing prepayment penalties on loans and penalties for early withdrawal of time deposits. Banks can make the penalties so severe that embedded option risks are practically eliminated. However, most banks have found customers resist paying large penalties and must reduce the penalties to more modest levels as a competitive strategy to attract additional business. This provides most banks with some protection if the movement in interest rates is not too large and occurs over a relatively long time period. However, if interest rates move sharply up or down within a short period of time, the modest penalties will provide little protection from the risk of customers exercising their options.

Yield Curve Risk

To begin an analysis of yield curve risk, it is important to define yield as it relates to the term "interest rate." When a new bond comes to market, it produces a stated rate of interest that is the market rate at that time. If the bond is sold at its face value (par value), the interest rate paid on the bond and the yield are identical. If interest rates move higher after the bond has been issued, the market value of the bond will be reduced so that the discount in price combined with the interest rate paid on the bond will produce a yield identical to the interest rate paid on newly issued bonds of a similar quality and maturity. Yield makes it possible to relate previously issued notes and bonds to the current level of interest rates. A yield curve is a line on a graph connecting the yields of all the maturities of the bonds of a particular issuer or quality rating (Figure 5.3). As the economy moves through the business cycle, the shape of the yield curve changes rather dramatically. During most of the business cycle, the yield curve has a positive slope: In other words, shorter term rates are lower than longer term rates. In Figure 5.3, line A illustrates a positively sloped Treasury yield curve that occurred on November 30, 1987. Later in the business cycle, when the Federal Reserve Bank slowed the economy by increasing short term interest rates, the yield curve became negatively sloped; that is to say shorter term rates were higher than longer term rates. A negatively sloped yield curve is frequently referred to as an inverted yield curve. Line B illustrates a negatively sloped Treasury yield curve that occurred on July 28, 1989. Yield curve risk occurs with the variations in yields between securities of differing maturities. In the examples in Figure 5.3, the difference in

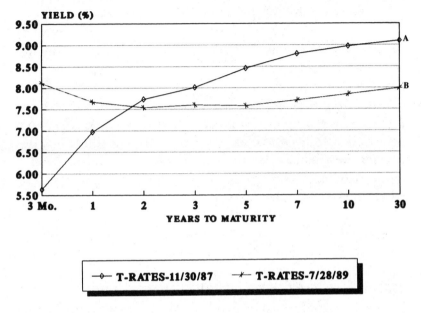

YIELD (%)

YEARS TO MATURITY

—◇— T-RATES-11/30/87   —✕— T-RATES-7/28/89

Figure 5.3 Positive and negative yield curves

the yield of a one-year Treasury bill and a 90-day Treasury bill when the yield curve is positive is 140 basis points. When the curve is inverted, the same maturities produce a negative spread of 42 basis points.

To illustrate how a change in the shape of the yield curve impacts a bank's net interest margin, let us assume that a bank has deliberately placed itself in a liability-sensitive gap position on November 30, 1987 by using 90-day term deposits to fund one year adjustable rate mortgages. If the bank pays 100 basis points above the 5.60% 90-day Treasury bill rate on its 90-day term deposits and charges 250 basis points above the one year Treasury bill rate of 7.00% on its

ARM's, a net interest spread of 290 basis points is produced (Table 5.12). By July 28, 1989, the yield curve has become inverted. The 90-day Treasury bill yield is 8.12% and the one-year Treasury bill yield is 7.70%. If the spread relationships of the deposits and loans to the Treasury rates remain constant, the net interest margin will be reduced to 108 basis points. This example is based on actual yield curves that have occurred within two years of each other and illustrates the impact on a bank's net interest margin that can occur if a bank maintains a mismatched gap position during a period when the shape of the yield curve changes.

Liquidity Risk

The ultimate risk in banking is the failure of the institution to have access to the cash it needs to meet deposit withdrawals or service its debt obligations. Therefore, it is vitally important for a bank to anticipate its near-term cash requirements and balance those demands against its potential sources of cash. The bank should be able to raise the cash quickly without incurring a substantial loss or costing an unreasonably high rate of interest.

Table 5.12 Yield Curve Risk

	Positive Yield Curve	Negative Yield Curve
1 Year ARM Rate	9.50%	10.20%
90-Day Term Deposit Rate	6.60%	9.12%
Net Interest Margin	2.90%	1.08%

Of all the risks inherent in financial arbitrage, that is to say banking, the one most difficult to measure is liquidity risk. The liquidity manager must anticipate the customer's future deposit activity; demand for loans; any change in the financial community's perception of the bank; changes in its competitive environment; and major developments in the local, state, national, and world economies. The manager must judge the impact these changes will have on the bank's liquidity requirements and structure the bank's assets and liabilities to provide the necessary liquidity.

The liquidity requirements of every bank are unique. No two banks have the same balance sheet composition, serve the same customer base, or operate in the same market areas. Since liquidity risk management involves highly subjective judgments unique to each institution, it is as much an art as a science. A detailed discussion of the analytical techniques enabling the liquidity risk manager to anticipate future liquidity requirements and identify appropriate funding sources will be presented in Chapter 8.

MEASURING THE RISKS

Before risks can be managed, they must first be identified and then quantified. Unless the amount of risk inherent in a financial institution's balance sheet can be measured, it is impossible to know the degree of risk to which an institution is exposed. It is also impossible to develop an effective risk management strategy without being able to understand the current risk position of the institution. The A/L manager must have the ability to measure the impact a risk management strategy will have on the institution's risk position.

Identifying and measuring all forms of risk is important to the A/L management process. The primary focus of the remainder of this chapter is measuring interest rate risk. Measuring liquidity risk and credit risk is discussed at length in Chapter 8.

An institution's interest rate risk position is the cumulative result of the thousands of individual deposits, loans, and investments comprising the balance sheet. Each deposit and loan has its own cash flow characteristics. To be fully aware of the risk inherent in an institution's balance sheet, one would need to comprehend every loan and deposit and relate their cash flows and repricing to a change in the general level of interest rates. Without the aid of a computer, this would be an impossible task.

Most asset/liability management software programs currently available in the market will produce a gap report. The gap report divides the repricing of the assets and liabilities into various time periods and determines whether there are more assets or liabilities repricing in any one period. Table 5.13 illustrates a typical gap report. In this example, the gap report indicates that during the first day of a change in interest rates, $100 million of assets will reprice while only $41 million of liabilities will reprice. This situation produces a positive one-day gap position of $59 million. In the next gap period (2 to 30 days) $38 million of liabilities will reprice while only $18 million of assets will reprice. This produces a negative gap position of $20 million during the 2-to-30-day period and creates a positive cumulative gap position through 30 days of $39 million. The $43 million negative gap in the 31-to-90-day period moves the cumulative gap through 90 days into negative territory by $4 million. The analysis continues in a like manner until the longest period is

Table 5.13 Gap Report ($ Millions)

Earning Assets	1 Day	2–30 Days	31–90 Days	91–365 Days	1–2 Years	2–5 Years	> Than 5 Years	Total
Federal Funds Sold	10	0	0	0	0	0	0	10
Floating Rate Securities	0	10	15	0	0	0	0	25
Fixed Rate Securities	0	0	5	20	25	20	10	80
1 Year ARMs	0	5	10	45	0	0	0	60
Fixed Rate Mortgages	0	1	2	9	13	52	80	157
Floating Rate Commercial Loans	60	0	0	0	0	0	0	60
Floating Rate Consumer Loans	30	0	0	0	0	0	0	30
Fixed Rate Consumer Loans	0	2	4	18	26	30	0	80
Total Assets Repricing in Each Period	100	18	36	92	64	102	90	502
Costing Liabilities								
Money Market Deposit Accounts	40	0	0	0	0	0	0	40
Regular Savings Accounts	0	0	1	3	5	15	35	59
90 Day CDs	1	14	30	0	0	0	0	45
180 Day CDs	0	10	20	30	0	0	0	60
1 Year CDs	0	8	16	72	0	0	0	96
2 Year CDs	0	4	8	36	48	0	0	96
3 Year CDs	0	2	4	18	24	24	0	72
Total Liabilities Repricing in Each Period	41	38	79	159	77	39	35	468
Gap Position in Each Period (Earning Assets − Costing Liabilities)	59	(20)	(43)	(67)	(13)	63	55	
Cumulative Gap Position	59	39	(4)	(71)	(84)	(21)	34	

completed. At that point, the cumulative gap position will reflect the net asset position of the institution. In the example in Table 5.13, the net asset position is a positive $34 million.

Any number of periods can be used when constructing a gap report. The more periods in the report, the more accurately the A/L manager can determine where the timing differences exist between the assets and liabilities. Most managers focus their attention on the near-term periods. It is the one-day gap period that immediately impacts the daily income statement. If management is concerned about quarterly earnings, the focus will be on the cumulative gap position through 90 days. At most institutions the emphasis is on annual earnings, so the focus is on the cumulative gap position through one year. For this reason when the term gap is used without specifying the period, it generally refers to the twelve month cumulative gap position. Longer gap periods receive less attention because it will be a relatively long time before they flow into the income statement. During that time there will be many changes in the balance sheet structure as well as opportunities to effect additional changes that will impact those specific gap positions. However, when focusing on longer-term horizons in the strategic planning process it is useful to carefully examine the longer-term gap periods.

The gap report informs the A/L manager about the general interest rate sensitivity position of the institution that arises from a mismatch in the repricing of assets and liabilities during any specific period. The report indicates whether the institution is positioned to benefit from rising interest rates by having a positive gap position or whether it is positioned to benefit from declining interest rates by its negative gap position. The size of the gap indicates the degree to which the institution will benefit from a favorable move in interest rates or suffer if interest rates move in a direction unfavorable to its gap position. In the example illustrated in Table 5.13, the institution has a cumulative 12-month gap position of negative $71 million. Therefore, this institution is positioned to benefit from a decline in interest rates during the next 12 months. The gap report also indicates the benefit of declining interest rates will be substantial because the $71 million represents 14% of the $502 million of total earning assets.

The gap report relates the balance sheet components directly to the institution's interest rate risk arising from the repricing differences of its assets and liabilities. This information is useful in understanding where an institution's rate risk is occurring and provides insight as to how the risk position can be changed. Examining the various asset and liability categories listed in Table 5.13 reveals that $55 million of the fixed-rate securities portfolio is invested longer than 12 months. This fact suggest a very effective strategy to reduce the negative gap position of this institution would be to sell the longer-term securities and invest the sale proceeds in securities with an interest rate sensitivity of less than one year.

Although the information provided by the gap report is useful and has been used as the primary measure of interest rate risk by numerous financial institutions for many years, gap reports fail to provide all the information necessary to measure an institution's total interest rate risk exposure. Gap quantifies the timing differences between the repricing of assets and liabilities but fails to measure the impact of basis risk and embedded options on the institution's interest rate risk position. Because gap fails to measure the total interest rate risk exposure, it cannot measure the entire impact a change in interest rates will have on an institution's net interest income or the effect a change in interest rates will have on the market value of an institution's assets and liabilities.

One of the basic principals of business is that management should strive to maximize the value of the firm. To do this, management must be able to measure the value of the firm and anticipate the effect interest rate risks and credit risks combined with their strategic plans will have on the future value of the institution. Bank regulators also need to measure the value of financial institutions for another reason. If the net value of portfolio equity, that is, the liquidation value of an institution is approaching zero, the regulators know they must act quickly to remedy the situation.

One approach to measuring the impact a change in interest rates will have on an institution's market value is net duration analysis. Duration is defined as the time-weighted average maturity of the present value of the cash flows generated by a financial instrument. Table 5.14 uses the example of a $10,000, 10%, five-year loan requiring annual interest payments to illustrate how duration is computed. The cash flows are discounted using the current market rate for five-year, fixed-rate loans to determine the present value of the cash flows. The present values are multiplied by the corresponding number of periods to obtain a time-weighted factor. Dividing the total of the time-weighted factors by the total of the present value of the cash flows produces the duration of the loan.

Table 5.14 Duration Calculation: 10%–$10,000 Loan with a Five-Year Maturity

Period in Years	Cash Flow	Present Value of Cash Flow at 10%	Weighted Present Value (Column 1 × Column 3)
1	1,000.00	909.09	909.09
2	1,000.00	826.45	1,652.90
3	1,000.00	751.31	2,253.93
4	1,000.00	683.01	2,732.04
5	11,000.00	6,830.14	34,150.70
Total		10,000.00	41,698.66

Duration = 41,698.61 ÷ 10,000 = 4.169861 Years

Duration directly links a change in interest rates to a change in the market value of a financial instrument. The equation that expresses that relationship is as follows:

$$\text{Percent price change} = \frac{(-D)}{(1 + Y)} (\Delta Y)(100)$$

D = Duration
Y = Discount rate used to determine the present value of the cash flows when computing the duration
ΔY = The Amount of change in interest rates from rate Y

Applying the equation to the example in Table 5.14 reveals that a decline in interest rates from 10% to 9% increases the value of the loan by 3.79% or $379.00. The calculations used to arrive at this conclusion are as follows:

$$\text{Percent price change} = \frac{(-4.169861)}{(1 + .10)} (-.01)(100) = 3.79\%$$

Change in the
  value of the loan = (original value)(percent price change)
            = ($10,000.00)(.0379) = $379.00

Duration can also be calculated for entire portfolios of financial instruments. Most sophisticated asset/liability management software systems have the ability to compute the duration of an institution's total asset structure as well as the duration of its total liability structure. The A/L manager can use the duration figures and the price and value equations to compute the change in value of the institution's assets and liabilities for any given change in interest rates. The difference between the duration of the asset structure and the duration of the liability structure is the institution's net duration. If the net duration is positive, that is, the duration of the assets is longer than the duration of the liabilities, a decrease in interest rates will increase the net value of the institution. Conversely, an increase in interest rates will decrease the net value of the institution. If the duration of an institution's asset structure matches that of its liability structure, the institution has immunized the risk, that is, the market value of the firm will remain constant when interest rates change.

Net duration analysis does not rely on interest rate forecasts because it is based on parallel shifts in the yield curve. For this reason, it fails to account for basis risks and changes in the shape of the yield curve. It also fails to adjust for accelerated prepayment of loans when rates decline sharply and the increase in early withdrawal of time deposits and the activation of ARM caps when interest rates rapidly increase. These actions alter the institution's cash flows and consequently change its net duration. The change in duration due to the activating of embedded options is referred to as convexity. Advanced A/L management software systems compute convexity factors by which duration is adjusted when extreme changes in interest rates activate the embedded options. Convexity adjustments improve the ability of duration analysis to more accurately measure the impact on the value of an institution's equity when interest rates change.

The most accurate estimate of the impact an interest rate change can have on an institution's market value is obtained by conducting a net present value analysis. This analysis determines the net present value of all the cash flows simulated by an asset/liability modeling system. A well-designed and carefully maintained modeling system will take into account embedded options and basis risks. Also, the model's ability to use various interest rate scenarios provides an opportunity to simulate changes in the shape of the yield curve. For these reasons the net present value analysis is used by most asset/liability modeling systems to derive an institution's market value of portfolio equity.

Asset/liability modeling systems are also used to conduct a dynamic simulation analysis that estimates the impact of interest rate risks on an institution's earnings. The analysis measures the overall performance of the institution under various interest rate scenarios and reports the results as projected income statements. By using the highest level to which interest rates could realistically move, the lowest level and management's best estimate of the future course of interest rates as the three primary interest rate scenarios, the

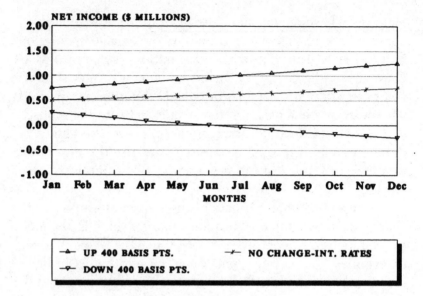

Figure 5.4 Dynamic simulation analysis results

A/L manager can measure the impact of interest rate risk as a range within which future earnings can be expected to occur unless specific action is taken to change the interest rate risk position of the institution. It is also a good idea to test additional interest rate scenarios that reflect changes in the slope of the yield curve. To help management understand the impact that interest rate risk can have on an institution's earnings, it is useful to visually summarize the results of the dynamic simulation analysis in a graphic format similar to that illustrated in Figure 5.4.

SUMMARY

To effectively identify and measure the magnitude of the interest rate risk to which an institution is exposed requires sophisticated computer software capable of modeling the institution and simulating the institution's future cash flows. The model must be able to produce gap reports, compute duration, determine the net value of portfolio equity, and simulate various interest rate scenarios. Although each approach to measuring interest rate risk has its limitations, synergy can be realized by utilizing the strengths of each approach.

Gap reports are useful to isolate areas of the balance sheet that constitute large portions of an institution's interest rate risk position caused by timing differences in the rate reset periods of assets and liabilities. The information contained in the gap reports often suggests various strategies for managing the interest rate risk. Net duration adjusted for convexity provides management with a single figure indicating the degree to which the value of the institution can change for a given change in interest rates. Knowing the duration of specific instruments or portfolios is also useful when constructing hedges. The impact of a change in interest rates on the value of the institution and its income is best measured by a computer modeling system capable of conducting a net present value analysis and a dynamic income simulation. These various measures of interest rate risk enable the asset/liability manager to identify and measure an institution's interest rate risk position and serve as financial tools to test the effectiveness of interest rate risk management strategies. In the deregulated banking environment of the 1990s, it is essential that A/L managers understand and manage the risks inherent in the balance sheet structure if their institutions are to survive as profitable and viable entities.

6

Managing Interest Rate Risk

BALANCE SHEET MANAGEMENT STRATEGIES FOR CONTROLLING INTEREST RATE RISK

To begin the interest rate risk management process, it is best to first use strategies that change the bank's interest rate sensitivity by altering various components of the balance sheet. Balance sheet management strategies are the basic tools of interest rate risk management. These strategies are familiar to most senior bank executives because they are the traditional tools that have been used by banks for many years. Altering a bank's interest rate risk exposure, simply stated, is creating an interest rate risk situation that will either counter or exacerbate the bank's existing interest rate risk exposure. A bank can get into serious financial difficulty if the members of the ALCO implement interest rate risk management strategies without fully understanding the impact their decisions can have on the bank's financial structure. Therefore, it is vitally important for all the members of the ALCO to understand the full impact of each strategy. That is why it is best to begin the interest rate risk management process by using strategies that are familiar to the senior management team.

Strategies Using the Investment Portfolio

One of the most basic balance sheet strategies to alter a bank's interest rate risk exposure is to sell fixed-income securities and reinvest the proceeds in securities with a different maturity. This is an effective way to quickly alter a bank's risk position by a significant amount. If a bank is too asset sensitive (more assets repricing in a given period than liabilities), the first course of action is to examine the shorter term maturities in the investment portfolio. The A/L manager must answer the following questions:

- Are the securities marketable?
- Are the securities pledged?
- What is the dollar amount of securities available for repositioning?
- Is senior management willing to book the resulting gain or loss?
- What is the yield of the securities based on their book value?
- What transaction costs are incurred?
- How will selling these securities impact the bank's liquidity position?

If it is determined that enough marketable securities are available for sale to significantly impact the risk position, management is willing to book the resulting gains or losses, the transaction costs incurred when selling the securities are not onerous, and selling the shorter-term securities will not adversely impact the bank's liquidity position, the A/L manager should proceed to examine the reinvestment possibilities.

One of the considerations when selecting a security to purchase with the proceeds from the sale of the shorter-term securities is its impact on the bank's risk position. If the bank's one-year gap position is determined to be too asset sensitive (more assets repricing in the next twelve months than liabilities), selling a Treasury bill with a 60-day maturity and reinvesting the proceeds in a Treasury bill maturing in 11 months will have no effect on the bank's one-year gap position. If the bank reinvests the sale proceeds in a Treasury note maturing in 13 months, the one-year gap imbalance is addressed for only one month. The asset sensitivity problem will reoccur the next month when the Treasury note moves to within 12 months of its maturity. The maturity of the new security should be substantially longer than the gap period being addressed.

The most effective way to determine an appropriate reinvestment maturity is to use an asset/liability modeling system to test the effect of various reinvestment maturities on the bank's gap position. A model with the capacity for dynamic gap analysis is extremely useful in conducting this test. If a model contains only a static gap analysis that reveals the various gap positions as viewed from the present time, reinvesting the sale proceeds in 13-month Treasury notes appears to reduce the asset sensitivity as measured by the one-year gap. When dynamic gap analysis is used to access the reinvestment strategy, the one-year gap position is viewed as it will appear in future periods and the folly of purchasing 13-month Treasury notes to reduce the asset-sensitive one-year gap position is revealed.

Another important consideration is the effect the sale and reinvestment will have on the bank's net interest margin. Selling a security that was purchased at some time in the past and reinvesting the proceeds at current interest rates will impact the bank's net interest margin. For example, if the bank purchased a five-year Treasury note three years ago when the rate on a five-year Treasury note was 9%, the note will continue to earn 9% for the next two years. If the bank's two-year gap position is too asset sensitive and it sells the

Treasury note at the current two year Treasury note rate of 7.5% and reinvests in a new five Year Treasury note yielding 8%, a 100 basis point reduction in the yield will occur for the next two years. Selling the 9% note at a time when two year Treasury note yields are 7.5% will produce a gain in the year in which the sale occurs. The extra 100 basis points of yield that would have been earned over the next two years (8% vs 9%) has been removed from the bank's net interest margin and is reported in the current year's income statement as a security gain. The effect is a 100 basis point reduction of the net interest margin on the securities for the next two years and a security gain that inflates the first year's net income at the expense of the second year's net income (see Table 6.1). If the impact on the net income in the second year is too much for the bank's senior management to accept, the A/L manager should explore the use of other strategies.

One way to offset the 100 basis point compression in the net interest margin is to reinvest in five-year securities issued by entities other than the U.S. Treasury. A five-year Agency note might yield 8.35% and a five-year 'A' rated corporate note 9%. Another way to offset the 100 basis point compression is available when the yield curve has a steeply positive slope. That is to say, the longer the maturity of a security, the higher the yield. Purchasing a seven-year Treasury note might yield 8.25% and a ten-year Treasury note might yield 8.5%. By combining these two approaches a bank might be able to enhance its net interest margin. It is acceptable banking practice to attempt to preserve some of the erosion in net interest margin by reinvesting in agencies and some high-quality corporate notes. However, the A/L committee must resist the temptation to push the investment manager

Table 6.1 Impact of Maturity Extension Program

Original $1 Million Investment Position

	Year 1	Year 2
Treasury Note @ 9%	90,000	90,000
Cost of Funding @ 7%	70,000	70,000
Net Interest Margin	20,000	20,000
Gain/(Loss) on Sale	–0–	–0–
Net Income (Pretax)	20,000	20,000

Maturity Extension Program

	Year 1	Year 2
Treasury Note @ 8%	80,000	80,000
Cost of Funding @ 7%	70,000	70,000
Net Interest Margin	10,000	10,000
Gain/(Loss) on Sale	27,385	–0–
Net Income (Pretax)	37,385	10,000

to purchase lower-quality and/or long-term securities in an attempt to bolster the net interest margin. In the past, some banks and many savings and loan associations yielded to this temptation and experienced disastrous results. During the 1980s many financial institutions invested in high-yielding long-term "junk bonds." For a few years, these securities significantly enhanced the bank's net interest margin. However, the recession that followed the economic expansion of 1982–89 produced numerous bankruptcies among the issuers of junk bonds. This resulted in large losses in the investment portfolios which, combined with substantial loan losses, caused many financial institutions to fail. A/L managers must continually be aware of one of the basic principles of finance, "the greater the return, the greater the risk." The fixed-income markets are very efficient at implementing this principle.

Another form of interest rate risk that can be addressed by redeploying the investment portfolio is basis risk. To become less liability sensitive, a bank could sell longer-term fixed-rate securities and purchase short-term fixed rate securities, or it could purchase long-term securities that have a floating interest rate. By selecting floating-rate securities that use an index rate that moves closely in tandem with a bank's cost of funding, the basis risk can be greatly reduced.

Many floating-rate securities use Treasury rates as their basis for resetting the interest rate on the security. The actual rate paid on the security is usually established at a fixed spread above the Treasury rate. If the bank's cost of funding does not change by the same amount as the change in the Treasury rates, variation in the net interest margin will occur. The only institution that can borrow at the Treasury rates is the Treasury. LIBOR and the prime rate will more closely reflect changes in a bank's cost of funds because they are indices used by banks when making loans. In most cases if floating-rate notes using LIBOR or prime as their index are selected as investments rather than floating-rate notes based on Treasury rates, the net interest margin will be better protected from compression due to an adverse shift in the basis relationship.

The investment portfolio cannot be managed in isolation from the rest of the bank. Although the investment officer's primary objective is to produce the maximum total return from the investment portfolio, the manager must do so within the constraints dictated by the bank's ALCO objectives. What might be a very shrewd strategy in a personal investment portfolio or pension fund portfolio could be totally inappropriate in the bank's portfolio. Consideration must be given to how an investment strategy impacts the bank's overall liquidity position, changes its interest rate risk, and affects its exposure to credit risk. It is essential for the A/L committee to communicate to the investment officers the bank's A/L objectives. The A/L manager must coordinate the actions of the departments within the bank that are responsible for managing various assets and liabilities if interest rate risk management strategies are to be effective.

Strategies Using Pricing and New Product Development

Many institutions with high levels of interest rate risk embedded in their balance sheet discover that the source of the risk has been the past pricing policies on loans and deposits. In the early 1980s, many savings and loan associations with pricing policies that had made them very liability sensitive, experienced massive losses when interest rates rose to record levels. For years, they had aggressively priced and marketed short-term deposits and used the deposits to fund thirty-year fixed-rate mortgages. It was only when rising interest rates began to create substantial losses that the pricing policies were changed.

To address this problem, creative bankers in conjunction with their Wall Street counterparts developed adjustable-rate mortgages with interest rates that reset every one, three, or five years. These were attractively priced and heavily marketed. To fund the new mortgages, depositors were enticed to extend the maturities of their deposits by high rates offered on time deposits with three-year and five-year maturities. By developing new loan and deposit products and aggressively pricing and marketing them, banks were able to create an arbitrage that produced a satisfactory net interest margin while incurring a low-level of interest rate risk.

The first base rate used as an index on the adjustable-rate mortgages was a Treasury instrument with the same maturity as the reset period. For example, the rate on a one-year adjustable-rate mortgage was based on a fixed spread above the prevailing one-year Treasury bill rate at the time of the reset. Although this addressed the gap problem it still left the banks exposed to considerable basis risk. To address this problem, the 11th Federal Home Loan Bank district, which encompasses numerous western states, began to publish the average cost of funds of its member banks. By using this rate as an index to reset mortgage rates, banks were able to reduce their basis risk by coupling the return on the adjustable-rate mortgages directly to their cost of funds rather than to the Treasury's cost of borrowing.

The major limitation of using pricing strategies to change an institution's interest rate risk exposure is that it takes a substantial period of time before it begins to significantly alter the total interest rate risk position. Many thrift institutions in the early 1980s had too much risk exposure and too little capital to survive long enough to benefit from their change in pricing strategies. Well thought out pricing policies on loans and deposits do not always provide a quick fix for an institution with too much interest rate risk exposure, but it is essential for maintaining the risk within acceptable parameters over the long term.

It is possible to accelerate the effects of a change in pricing strategies by paying above-market rates on deposits and charging below-market rates on new loans. It is also possible, although not advisable, to encourage new lending activity by relaxing the credit standards for new borrowers. New England thrift institutions had, for over one hundred years, confined their lending activity to financing residential real estate. With the deregulation of the financial system in the early 1980s, they saw an opportunity to reduce their heavily liability-sensitive balance sheet positions by making large amounts of floating rate commercial loans. At first they competed for new commercial loans by offering aggressive rates, but as the competition for new business became more intense, credit requirements at some institutions were relaxed. The strategy worked very well. The liability-sensitive positions were sharply reduced as the thrifts booked large amounts of floating-rate commercial loans. The net interest margins suffered a little as the cost of funds increased while aggressively low rates were charged on the commercial loans, but the increased volume of activity enabled the bank's net income to continue to expand. However, when the business cycle moved into a recession, the relaxed credit standards produced massive loan losses. A/L managers must be aware of the impact their strategies have on the bank's credit risk exposure.

The new product development manager, those responsible for establishing the rates on loans and deposits, and the marketing department must be aware of the asset/liability management objectives of the bank. It is the responsibility of the ALCO to keep them informed so they can design pricing policies for deposits and loans, develop new loan and deposit products, and focus the bank's marketing effort to achieve the ALCO's objectives. Effective product pricing, new product development, and focused marketing programs are essential for managing interest rate risk and improving the net interest margin over the long term.

Strategies Using Loan Sales and Purchases

The loan portfolios had never been considered very liquid components of the balance sheet until the late 1970s when Wall Street developed several new financial instruments that converted banks' loan portfolios into marketable securities. In the 1970s, various government-sponsored agencies were established to encourage mortgage lending. They were GNMA (Government National Mortgage Association), FNMA (Federal National Mortgage Association) and FHLMC (Federal Home Loan Mortgage Corporation). These agencies guaranteed blocks of one-to-four family mortgages that met their criteria and that were submitted on their standardized forms. No longer must the investor be concerned with the value, condition, and location of each mortgaged property because the agencies guarantee the payment of principal and interest. Banks can gather individual mortgages into a large pool, submit it to one of the agencies and receive an agency-guaranteed security representing owner-ship of the pool. The security is readily marketable because it trades in the market as a generic security with all other mortgage pools guaranteed by the same agency with an identical coupon. In addition to being readily marketable, these securities can be pledged for various purposes and can be used as collateral for borrowing and repurchase agreements.

The concept of gathering individual loans into large pools and adding credit enhancements to create a marketable security has now advanced beyond the mortgage portfolio. In

1985, Saloman Brothers issued the first security backed by the cash flows produced by a pool of automobile loans. They named the instrument Certificates of Automobile Receivables or CARs for short. If a bank wants to securitize and sell part of its automobile loan portfolio, there are now several brokerage firms that will purchase the loans to create CARs or if the portfolio is large enough, create a CAR for the bank.

CARs are excellent investment vehicles for banks with excess funds to invest because they offer a significant spread above the two-year Treasury note yield, have an average maturity of 1.5 to 2.5 years, are secured by the cash flows resulting from the pool of automobile loans, and include credit enhancements. For example, GMAC sells its automobile loans in the form of CARs with the agreement to repurchase defaulted loans amounting to 5% of the aggregate amount of the issue. The spread advantage of CARs above the two-year Treasury note rate has ranged from 60 to 80 basis points.

The most recent type of securitized loan instrument is the CARD. These are securities backed by the cash flows resulting from a portfolio of credit card loans. They bear more risk than securities backed by mortgages or automobile loans because they are unsecured and experience a higher delinquency rate. To compensate the investor for this risk, the issuing bank will frequently guarantee to reimburse the investor for losses up to 10% of the gross portfolio. The average maturity of CARDs is 1.5 to 2.0 years and their yield advantage over a two-year Treasury note has ranged from 80 to 120 basis points.

The ability to securitize loans is a valuable tool for the A/L manager. It greatly increases the liquidity of the bank's balance sheet and, in the case of mortgages, enables the bank to retain the mortgages on the balance sheet and eliminate the credit risk inherent in those mortgages by paying a small guarantee fee to one of the federal agencies.

Loan securitization also enables the banks to make loans on terms demanded by the customer but that might be inappropriate for the bank to retain in its loan portfolio given its interest rate risk parameters. For example, most banks do not want to hold a large portfolio of 30-year fixed rate mortgages. However, there is a large consumer demand for those mortgages. By making the thirty-year fixed-rate mortgages, converting them to agency guaranteed securities, and immediately selling them in the securities market, the bank can meet their customers' demands for 30 year fixed-rate mortgages without incurring additional interest rate risk. A further advantage of securitizing and selling loans is that it enables banks to satisfy a large volume of loan demand in their service area that may be far greater than their ability to fund through the bank's normal deposit-gathering activity.

Every bank should explore the possibility of securitizing its various loan portfolios. Even if the bank decides it does not want to securitize any of its portfolios at the present time, it should begin to use the standardized loan forms and procedures so that it will have the option to securitize the loans at some future date. The ability to securitize loans is an essential tool that must be available to A/L managers if they are to have the flexibility required to effectively manage their bank's liquidity position and interest rate risks.

Strategies Using Brokered Deposits

Just as Wall Street applied its inventiveness to the asset side of the balance sheet by creating securitized loans, it also addressed the liability side of the balance sheet by developing the brokered deposit market. Traditionally, regional and local banks could obtain new deposits only by aggressively pricing and marketing deposit products in their service area. Problems often arose when two or more banks in a particular region would begin to aggressively compete for funds by offering successively higher interest rates on deposits. This action forced the other banks servicing the region to increase deposit rates in order to maintain their share of the deposit market. As a result, the banks' cost of funds increased and caused a compression in the banks' net interest margins.

Deposits are frequently slow to respond in any meaningful dollar amount to deposit pricing and marketing of traditional deposit gathering activities. If a bank has a large funding need or wants to alter its interest rate risk posture, it is forced to offer an interest rate substantially above the market rate in order to more rapidly attract a significant amount of new deposits. Generally, there is some rate that will attract new deposits in size but the question is whether or not the bank is willing or able to pay it. In the 1980s, many banks wanted to extend the average maturity of their deposit structure by enticing depositors to move into five-year CDs. However, the banks discovered the consumer required an interest rate premium to lock in a long-term deposit rate that was much higher than most banks were willing to pay. As a result, many banks added only very small amounts of five-year CDs to their balance sheets.

Another problem with traditional deposit gathering activities is cannibalizing the existing deposit base. Programs to attract new deposit dollars are sometimes so aggressively marketed and attractively priced that a significant amount of the bank's existing low-cost deposit base transfers into the new higher-yielding deposit instrument. This causes the bank's average cost of funds to increase, which reduces the net interest margin.

To address these problems, brokerage firms used their retail offices to develop a nationwide market for regional bank CDs. For fees ranging from 25 basis points to 60 basis points of the principal amount of the deposits, retail brokerage firms can quickly obtain millions of dollars in time deposits for regional banks. This enables banks to very rapidly attract large amounts of new time deposits without cannibalizing the existing deposit base and provides an alternative funding source for banks caught in the crossfire of a regional deposit rate war.

There are many different types of brokered deposit programs, so each bank must shop the various brokerage firms to see what is most appropriate for their requirements. Not only do the fees and interest rates vary widely, but the accounting system and depositor base also vary. Some retail brokers market the CDs to individual retail clients up to the limit insured by the FDIC. The hundreds of resulting individual accounts must be accounted for separately on a special accounting system developed by the broker. Other deposit brokers sell a few very large CDs directly to institutional investors such as pension funds, insurance companies, and other banks. A bank must take into consideration variations in the capital requirements, the different deposit insurance expense, and the operating costs of these two alternatives.

Banks must resist the temptation to develop a heavy reliance on brokered deposits. If the banking industry enters a period of difficulty or if an individual bank encounters problems, the bank may be forced to pay a hefty interest rate premium to attract buyers for its CDs. In extreme situations, a bank could be totally denied access to the CD market. A bank too heavily dependent on the brokered CD market would then experience a sharp increase in its cost of funds, or in the latter case, encounter a liquidity crisis. Every bank should have as part of its ALCO policy a provision that places a limit on the amount of brokered deposits it can have outstanding at any point in time. The role of brokered deposits in the A/L management process is to enhance deposit strategies and must not be relied on as a major source of permanent funding.

Strategies Using Borrowed Funds

Bank borrowings fall into two general categories, short-term borrowings and long-term borrowings. Each of these categories of borrowings serves a very different function in the asset/liability management process. The traditional role of short-term borrowings is to make up the shortfall in the bank's cash flows resulting from daily fluctuations or seasonal cash flow patterns. However, short-term borrowing can also be used in an asset/liability management strategy as a source of interest-sensitive funding that can be created quickly and in large amounts.

The two most common sources of short-term borrowings are the purchase of federal funds and the use of reverse repurchase agreements. Purchased federal funds are usually an overnight inter-bank unsecured loan that must be paid back on the next business day. Occasionally, a bank can strike a deal with a federal funds lender to borrow at a fixed rate of interest for up to 90 days. These are referred to as term federal funds borrowings. Federal funds should not be relied on as a permanent source of funding. Even if a bank has had a satisfactory borrowing relationship with a lending agent for many years, the request to borrow federal funds can be declined. In the 1989–92 period, some banks' requests to borrow federal funds were denied as their financial condition deteriorated. For this reason, banks should establish federal fund borrowing lines with several banks and not rely on federal funds as a source of permanent funding.

A reverse repurchase agreement (reverse repo) is the sale of securities with a simultaneous agreement to repurchase them at a fixed price on a specific date. The terms of the agreement are structured such that the borrower of the funds pays the lender a rate of interest for the use of the funds. The interest rate, established when the reverse repo agreement is entered into, is usually slightly below the federal funds rate. Although the securities are delivered to the lender and the reverse repo is an agreement to sell securities and buy them back at a later date, the transaction is recorded as a secured borrowing and not as a sale of the securities.

There are three basic kinds of reverse repurchase agreements. Overnight reverse repo's are the equivalent of purchasing federal funds. The bank sends the securities to the dealer and the dealer sends the funds to the bank. The next business day, the bank returns the funds plus interest to the dealer and the dealer returns the securities. When a bank intends to roll overnight reverse repos for at least several days, an open reverse repo may be more convenient. As with an overnight reverse repo, the bank sends the dealer the securities in return for funds. However, the dealer does not automatically unwind the reverse repo the next day. The dealer will call the bank, inform the investment officer what the rate will be for that day, and the bank can decide whether or not to continue the reverse repo for another day. An open reverse repo eliminates the confusion that can result from rolling overnight reverse repo's and passing the collateral back and forth each day. The third kind of reverse repo is the term reverse repo. These are reverse repurchase agreements entered into for longer periods of time, generally three days to six months. The primary advantage of using term repos is the assured availability of the funds and a fixed rate during the term of the agreement.

The credit risk in using reverse repos as short-term funding vehicles arises from the fact that the dealer does not lend the full market value of the security. For example, if the current market value of a security is $10 million of principal and $400,000 of accrued interest, the dealer will lend the bank $10,300,000 rather than the $10,400,000 total value. If the dealer were to default on the agreement, the bank would lose $100,000. Although the amount at risk is small relative to the underlying amount of the transaction, it is always a good idea to enter into reverse repos only with reputable, well-capitalized banks and brokerage firms.

During times of stress in the banking system, when federal funds borrowing lines may be canceled, banks can usually generate short-term funds by using Treasury securities for reverse repurchase agreements. It greatly enhances the asset/liability manager's ability to generate funds for short-term liquidity needs to have Treasury securities available for reverse repos. To accomplish this, the investment portfolio manager should not use Treasury securities for pledging purposes unless required to do so by the party demanding the pledging. If Treasury securities are currently being used for pledging purposes, the party requiring the pledge should be contacted to see if securitized mortgages or some other type of security can be substituted for the Treasuries.

Long-term borrowings are an attractive source of funds to banks. They provide the bank an opportunity to establish a fixed rate of interest on borrowed funds for long periods of time and they reduce the bank's liquidity risk. When short-term debt matures, the bank must either generate enough funds to retire the debt or expose itself to the ever-shifting preferences of the securities markets and hope that investors will be willing to again purchase the short-term debt of the issuing bank. By issuing long-term debt the problem of rolling over the debt is deferred into the distant future.

Another advantage of using long-term debt is the opportunity to lock in an interest rate that will remain fixed during the term of the debt. However, locking in the rate is only one option. Almost any type of intermediate or long-term debenture can be issued with either a fixed rate or floating rate. It does not matter whether a bank is too asset sensitive or too liability sensitive, it can use long-term debt to reduce its interest rate risk exposure while it reduces its liquidity risks. A bank can reduce its asset sensitivity by issuing floating-rate long-term debt or it can reduce its liability sensitivity by issuing long-term fixed-rate debt.

A problem arises for small and medium-sized banks because long-term debt issues are usually brought to market by investment bankers, so the size of the issue must be quite large to justify the underwriting fees and expenses. Also, smaller banks may find it difficult to profitably reinvest the huge amount of funds generated by such a large debt issue. The Federal Home Loan Bank and the Student Loan

Marketing Association provide an alternative to these banks by allowing them to borrow smaller amounts on a secured basis at fixed rates for varying periods of time.

Long-term debt can be issued in many forms. A common form of unsecured long-term debt is debentures. Debentures are listed as debt in the liability section of the balance sheet, but are considered as capital by the regulators because the owners of the debentures have an unsecured position. Another advantage of the debenture is that the interest expense is deductible against taxable income. A recent variation on the debenture concept is the deposit note, which is basically an intermediate term debenture.

Preferred stock is a hybrid form of long-term debt. Like debentures, preferred stock is a long-term debt instrument that does not dilute the common stock ownership of the bank and it can be issued with either a fixed or floating interest rate. However, unlike debentures, the interest is referred to as a dividend and is paid from the aftertax earnings of the bank. Although this is a disadvantage for a profitable bank it is partially offset by the fact that corporate investors are willing to accept a relatively low rate of interest on preferred stock because the dividends are 70% exempt from federal corporate income taxes. Each bank must weigh the advantage of the low dividend rate it will pay on preferred stock against the fact that the dividend must be paid from aftertax dollars to determine whether preferred stock is an appropriate long-term debt vehicle.

To facilitate issuing long-term debt, it is helpful to be assigned a rating from one of the bank rating services such as Moody's, Standard and Poor's, or Thomson BankWatch Service. A satisfactory rating from one of these services may enable the bank to issue the debt at a lower interest rate than would otherwise be the case. A satisfactory rating will also facilitate borrowing federal funds, issuing brokered deposits, establishing correspondent relationships, or any other activity that would require an analysis of the bank's financial condition.

Summary

Most effective asset/liability managers rely on many strategies for managing a bank's interest rate risk. They often employ several strategies at the same time. To determine which strategies are the most appropriate, the asset/liability managers must ask the following questions of each strategy:

- How does it affect the bank's gap position?
- Does it increase or decrease the bank's basis risk?
- What is the effect on the net interest margin when tested against various interest rate scenarios?
- Will it generate a gain or a loss?
- How does it affect the bank's liquidity position?
- Does it expand the bank's balance sheet?
- What is the maximum or minimum dollar amount that can be efficiently transacted?
- How quickly can it be accomplished?
- What are the transaction costs?

Tables 6.2 and 6.3 present a summary of the various balance sheet strategies for reducing asset sensitivity and for reducing liability sensitivity. The tables summarize the liquid-

Table 6.2 Various Strategies for Reducing Asset Sensitivity

Description	Source or Use of Funds	Will it Expand The Balance Sheet?
Extend Investment Portfolio Maturities	—	No
Increase Floating-Rate Deposits	Source	Yes
Increase Short-Term Deposits	Source	Yes
Increase Fixed-Rate Lending	Use	Yes
Sell Adjustable-Rate Loans	Source	No
Increase Short-Term Borrowings	Source	Yes
Increase Floating-Rate Long-Term Debt	Source	Yes

Table 6.3 Various Strategies for Reducing Liability Sensitivity

Description	Source or Use of Funds	Will it Expand The Balance Sheet?
Reduce Investment Portfolio Maturities	—	No
Increase Longer-Term Deposits	Source	Yes
Increase Adjustable-Rate Lending	Use	Yes
Sell Fixed-Rate Loans	Source	No
Increase Fixed-Rate Long-Term Debt	Source	Yes

ity impact of each strategy by noting those that are a source of cash and those that are a use of cash. If a bank wants to reduce its asset-sensitive position by making more fixed-rate loans, it must determine an appropriate strategy to fund them. That is why many asset/liability managers combine strategies such as increasing fixed-rate lending (a use of funds) with increasing variable-rate deposits (a source of funds).

The third column of Tables 6.2 and 6.3 indicates which strategies have the potential to expand a bank's balance sheet. Marginally capitalized banks will want to avoid strategies that will expand the balance sheet. If they have marginal capital, they may even want to shrink the balance sheet.

Each strategy and combination of strategies must be tested using the bank's asset/liability modeling system. Every bank has a unique balance sheet structure and serves different market areas. What may be the optimal combination of strategies to reduce asset sensitivity at one institution may not be appropriate to reduce asset sensitivity at another institution. A strategy examined as an isolated event may appear to be the best strategy; however, when integrated into the bank's balance sheet using the A/L model, its overall impact may prove unsatisfactory. This is why it is critically important to select a well-designed model, know how to operate it, accurately input the data and carefully and thoughtfully design the various test scenarios.

A major risk that cannot be measured by the A/L models is credit risk. The A/L manager must ferret out the credit risk of each strategy and inform the Asset/Liability Management Committee of the risk. The committee can then decide whether the bank is willing to incur the risk and if it is, develop policies and procedures to manage and monitor the risk. A great temptation for banks is to downgrade the credit quality of their loans and investments as they strive to enhance the bank's net interest income. In the short run, this strategy will work very well. However, when the business cycle turns, as it inevitably will, the resulting losses may often eliminate the incremental yield advantage and could result in significant loan charge-offs.

The balance sheet strategies described in this chapter are essential tools for managing interest rate risk. Asset/liability managers must have them available to use if they are to have the flexibility required to effectively manage the bank's liquidity and interest rate risks. Even though a bank may be perfectly satisfied with its current interest rate risk posture, the A/L manager should take action to be sure the bank stands ready to implement these strategies if the need arises. The A/L manager must educate the members of the ALCO so they completely understand the full impact of the various strategies. The committee should then develop policies and procedures for the strategies it deems most appropriate. Where special relationships are required such as deposit brokers to sell the bank's CDs, the A/L manager should begin searching for reputable firms that will do an effective job of marketing the bank's CDs. It costs nothing to put the agreements and procedures in place. Most costs are incurred when the strategy is implemented. This process, from educating the committee to selecting brokers and investment bankers, if done well, requires time. The A/L manager must not wait until the need arises to begin the process.

To effectively implement balance sheet strategies the A/L manager must have the ability to coordinate the activities of the various departments that are responsible for managing each section of the balance sheet. If the asset/liability management committee decides more short-term deposits are needed, the A/L manager must instruct the marketing department to promote short-term deposits and instruct those responsible for deposit pricing to aggressively price short-term deposits. The A/L manager must also be sure the bank's investment officers understand the bank's asset/liability objectives and tailor their investment activity accordingly. Managing interest rate risks using balance sheet strategies will be only marginally successful if the A/L manager is not able to coordinate the activities of the various departments within the bank.

OFF BALANCE SHEET MANAGEMENT STRATEGIES FOR CONTROLLING INTEREST RATE RISK

Asset/Liability managers have many strategies from which to choose when developing a plan to alter the interest rate risk of their institutions. The strategies range from very traditional approaches, such as changing the maturity structure of the investment portfolio, to strategies involving the use of more innovative instruments, such as interest rate swaps. Most bankers are comfortable with the more traditional approaches to interest rate risk management because they involve manipulating the elements that comprise the bank's balance sheet. However, senior management's level of comfort diminishes rapidly when strategies involving off balance sheet products are recommended. This is unfortunate because off balance sheet products sometimes are the most effective way to address certain interest rate risk management problems. Also, off balance sheet products do not materially leverage the balance sheet and can be put into place quickly. When necessary, they can be done in substantial size so as to have a significant impact on the bank's interest rate risk exposure without effecting the bank's liquidity position.

Off balance sheet products are frequently referred to as synthetic instruments. Although they do not appear on the balance sheet, they can have a major impact on the bank's net interest income during periods of rapidly changing interest rates. The three basic types of synthetic instruments used to manage interest rate risks are financial futures, interest rate swaps, and caps and floors.

Financial Futures

A financial future contract is a commitment between two parties in which the first party agrees to sell the second party a certain amount of a generic financial instrument, at a specific price, on a designated future date. If interest rates decline before the future delivery date, the value of the futures contract will go up because the value of the underlying financial instrument will increase. At the end of each trading day, the clearing house (an organization established by various brokerage firms to settle futures transactions) confirms the value of each futures contract. If the value of the contract goes up during the day, the seller must pay the buyer the amount of the daily increase. Conversely, if the value of the contract declines, the buyer must pay the seller the amount by which the value of the contract has declined. This process is referred to as a margin call. The margin is cleared daily to prevent the party that is experiencing a loss on the contract from accumulating a large loss that they might be unable to pay.

To illustrate how an asset-sensitive bank can use futures to reduce its exposure to a change in interest rates, consider the following example. A bank expects interest rates to decline 100 basis points during the next six months. Using its advanced asset/liability modeling system, which takes into consideration basis risk and embedded options as well as gap, it has determined a 100 basis point decline in interest rates will cause the net interest income to shrink by $250,000. The ALCO instructs the asset/liability manager to use futures to hedge this risk. Because most of the margin compression in financial institutions occurs due to a decline in short-term interest rates such as the prime rate, commercial paper rates, and adjustable-rate mortgages based on the one-year Treasury bill rate, the asset/liability manager will use a six-month futures contract based on the 91-day Treasury bill rather than one based on the 20-year Treasury bond, or a 30-year fixed-rate GNMA security to hedge the risk. A 100 basis point decline in interest rates will produce a $2,500 increase in the value of a $1 million, 91-day Treasury bill futures contract. To offset the $250,000 compression in the net interest income, the A/L manager must purchase 100 contracts.

There are several risks involved in this type of hedge. The most obvious risk occurs when interest rates increase rather than decrease. If the 91-day Treasury bill rate increased 100 basis points, a $250,000 loss would occur in the futures contract. The bank, having model-tested its futures hedge against various worse-case scenarios, knows that a 100 basis point increase in short-term interest rates will increase the bank's net interest income $250,000 because of its asset-sensitive balance sheet structure. If the hedge is put in place, the current net interest margin will be assured no matter which direction interest rates move during the next six months. A loss generated by the futures position will be offset by an improvement in the bank's net interest margin.

It is essential for the senior bank managers and bank regulators to evaluate the impact of a movement in interest rates on a synthetic instrument in the context of the total balance sheet and not in isolation. When interest rates increase 100 basis points, the resulting $250,000 loss in the futures contract makes it seem as though the A/L manager has made a very bad decision. However, when the effect of the rate increase on the bank's entire balance sheet is included in the analysis, it becomes evident the loss on the futures contract is offset by the increase in the bank's net interest income. The A/L manager has not committed a grave error, but has created an effective hedge that preserves the bank's net interest income. Senior bank managers and regulators must resist the tendency to examine synthetic instruments in isolation from the rest of the balance sheet.

A more subtle risk in this hedge is the basis risk arising from the cross-hedge (hedging one instrument with a contract based on another). The value of the futures contract is based on the change of the 91-day Treasury bill interest rate. However, the change in the bank's net interest margin is due to changes in the prime lending rate, commercial paper rates, and the one-year Treasury bill rate. The 91-day Treasury bill rate could move 75 basis points before causing a 50 basis point change in the prime lending rate. A change in the shape of the yield curve could also cause some inefficiency in the hedge. For example, the 91-day Treasury bill rate might increase more rapidly than the one-year Treasury bill rate, creating a loss on the 91-day Treasury bill futures contracts that would more than offset the resulting gain on adjustable mortgage rates based on the one-year Treasury bill rate.

The risk of overhedging or underhedging exists because loan prepayments, new lending activity, deposit shifts, and security sales cause constant changes in the bank's interest rate risk exposure. It is essential for the A/L manager to frequently update the asset/liability computer model and test the interest rate risk position of the bank's balance sheet against the hedging instruments to determine whether an adjustment in the hedge is warranted.

Using futures to hedge the interest rate risk in the balance sheet is like mixing apples with pears. What is being hedged is a change in the difference between the interest income generated by a group of assets and the interest expense of a group of liabilities due to a change in interest rates. The hedge is based on the change in the market value of a particular financial instrument as a result of the same interest rate change during the same time period. This is why it is important that financial futures not be employed as an interest rate risk management tool unless the A/L manager is extremely knowledgeable about the bank's interest rate risk exposure and is thoroughly familiar with the various financial futures instruments and markets.

Interest Rate Swaps

An interest rate swap is an agreement between two parties to exchange a stream of interest payments during a designated future period. Because it is an exchange of interest payments and involves no principal payments, it is a very direct way to alter the interest rate being paid or received on a financial instrument or hedge fluctuations in the net interest margin that result when changes in interest rates cause variations in a bank's stream of interest income and interest expense.

The credit risk of an interest rate swap lies in the possibility that the other party to the agreement may be unable to make the net interest payments if the swap goes against them. This is why it is an important first step when starting to use swaps to select reputable, well-capitalized commercial banks or investment banks that are major participants in the swap market. It is wise to use several institutions when purchasing swaps because it will enable the purchasing bank to shop the rates at various institutions and provide issuer diversification in the swap portfolio. The purchasing bank must also be sure the issuing bank is standing as principal, not as agent. If the bank is acting as agent, it has no direct responsibility for the interest payments to be made in a timely manner.

The most commonly used interest rate swap is the fixed versus floating swap. One party to the swap agrees to pay a fixed rate of interest on a hypothetical principal amount, referred to as the notional amount, and the other party to the agreement agrees to pay a variable interest rate, usually 90-day LIBOR (London Inter Bank Offering Rate) on the same notional amount. The fixed rate of interest will remain unchanged during the term of the agreement, which usually ranges from two to ten years and will be paid every six months. The 90-day LIBOR rate will be paid every 90 days at which time the rate will be adjusted to match the then-current 90-day LIBOR rate.

There are two general types of interest rate risk hedges in which swaps can be used: transaction hedges and balance sheet hedges. In a transaction hedge, a swap is used to alter the interest rate characteristics of a specific transaction, such as transforming a fixed-rate loan to a floating-rate basis. If a bank's customers are demanding five-year fixed-rate loans at a time when the bank does not want to increase its liability sensitivity by making fixed-rate loans, it can accommodate the customer's demand for fixed-rate loans without increasing its liability sensitivity by using an interest rate swap. For example, if the First National Bank makes $25 million of five-year fixed-rate loans at a yield of 11%, it can change the loan into a variable-rate loan by entering into an interest rate swap agreement for a notional amount of $25 million in which it pays an 8.5% fixed rate of interest for a period of five years and receives a variable 90-day LIBOR rate for the next five years. Thus, the rate received on the loan has been converted to a variable rate 250 basis points above 90-day LIBOR (11.0%–8.5% + 90 day LIBOR) (Figure 6.1).

The major risk in the transaction hedge lies in the possibility the borrower will pay off the loan prior to the five-year maturity date. If the payoff occurred at a time when interest rates had moved sharply lower, it would cost the bank a substantial amount of money to unwind the swap. This is why it is important to charge substantial prepayment penalties on any loans that are hedged by swaps.

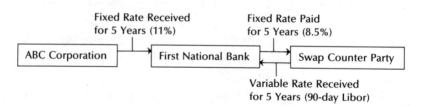

Figure 6.1 Transaction hedge using a swap to convert a fixed rate loan into a variable rate loan

Interest rate swaps can also be used to alter the interest rate characteristics of deposits; however, changing the interest rate flows of the deposit structure can create some additional risk. Maturity risk occurs when a deposit matures and the depositor has the option to withdraw the deposit. However, maturity risk is not a problem when a bank is converting long-term fixed-rate deposits to floating-rate deposits by receiving a fixed rate of interest on a swap and paying 90-day LIBOR. Figure 6.2 presents an example where the First National Bank is paying 9% on a block of $10 million five-year CDs. By entering into a swap for a notional amount of $10 million in which the bank receives a fixed rate of 8.5% for five years and agrees to pay 90-day LIBOR on a floating basis, the bank has transformed the five-year fixed-rate deposit into a variable-rate five-year deposit that will cost the bank 50 basis points above the 90-day LIBOR rate (9% − 8.5% + 90-day LIBOR). If the bank has a substantial penalty for early deposit withdrawals, the transaction hedge should work very well.

If the bank wants to increase the amount of five-year fixed-rate deposits by $10 million, but the depositors' prefer-

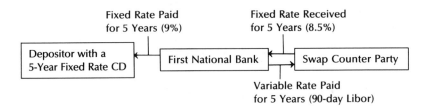

Figure 6.2 Transaction hedge using a swap to convert a fixed rate deposit into a floating rate deposit

ence is for 90-day fixed-rate deposits, the bank would be exposed to maturity risk if it entered into a swap in which it received a variable 90-day LIBOR rate and paid a fixed rate of interest for five years. The maturity risk occurs because the depositors can, without penalty, refuse to renew their 90-day deposits. A/L managers must be aware of the risk and hedge the position only to the extent of the core 90-day deposit base that is expected to be maintained at all times during the next five years. Figure 6.3 presents an example of a bank that converted a $10 million core holding of 90 day deposits into five year fixed rate deposits by entering into a $10 million interest rate swap in which the bank pays an 8.5% fixed rate of interest for five years and receives a variable 90 day LIBOR rate.

Another risk inherent in the above examples is basis risk. In the example described in Figure 6.1 the fixed rate on a loan was converted to a floating LIBOR rate. Although 90-day LIBOR and the bank's cost of funds will move in the same direction as the change in the general level of interest rates, they will probably not change by the same amount.

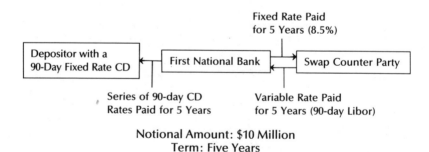

Figure 6.3 Transaction hedge using a swap to convert a series of core 90-day deposits into a five year fixed rate deposit

Banks can employ swaps to manage the gap position, but basis risk will continue to cause variations in the net interest margin.

To construct a balance sheet hedge using swaps that will address basis risks, maturity risks, and gap risks, the A/L manager must use an asset/liability modeling system. The A/L manager must carefully construct various interest rate scenarios and project the changes that can occur in the bank's balance sheet then measure their impact on the net interest income. When constructing a hedge employing interest rate swaps, the A/L manager must determine the positive and negative net interest amount that would be generated by a $1 million swap under the same rate scenarios used in the model. By dividing the change in the net interest income by the amount of the net interest income generated by the $1 million swap under each interest rate scenario, the A/L manager can determine the notional amount of swaps required to hedge the interest rate risk of each scenario.

Table 6.4 illustrates an example of a bank in which the net interest income decreases as interest rates decline. The net interest income experiences a constant $550,000 change for each 100 basis point movement in interest rates except for interest rate changes of 300 and 400 basis points. Under these scenarios margin compression begins to accelerate as interest rates decline. This situation commonly occurs in financial institutions when a large decline in interest rates occurs. Conversely, net interest income tends to expand as interest rates rise. This occurs because the interest rates paid on deposits increase less than the general rise in the level of interest rates and decline less than the general level of interest rates when rates fall.

An appropriate balance sheet hedge to reduce the negative

Table 6.4 Amount of Swaps Required to Hedge the Net Interest Income Decline

Rate Scenario	Change in the Bank's Net Interest Income (NII)	Annual Net Interest Cash Flow of a $1 Million Swap	Amount of Swaps Required to Hedge NII Decline
−400 Basis Points	−3,000,000	+40,000	75,000,000
−300	−2,000,000	+30,000	67,000,000
−200	−1,100,000	+20,000	55,000,000
−100	− 550,000	+10,000	55,000,000
No Change	–0–	–0–	–0–
+100	+ 550,000	−10,000	–0–
+200	+1,100,000	−20,000	–0–
+300	+2,000,000	−30,000	–0–
+400	+3,000,000	−40,000	–0–

effect a decline in interest rates will have on the bank's net interest income is a swap in which the bank pays a variable rate of interest and receives a fixed rate. The term of the swap is normally determined by the bank's interest rate forecast and structural changes in the bank's balance sheet that are expected to occur during the period encompassed by the rate forecast. In the current example, the bank's management is not expecting any major changes in the composition of the bank's balance sheet during the next few years; however, it does expect interest rates to decline for the next 24 months. To bridge the expected decline in interest rates, the A/L manager could select a swap with a three-year term.

If the 90-day LIBOR rate is 9% and the fixed rate received on a three-year swap is also 9% at the time the swap agreement is put in place, there will be no initial cost of hedging. However, as interest rates change, net interest cash flows will be generated by the swap. The resulting cash flows for a $1 million swap, where the bank pays a fixed rate of 9% and receives 90-day LIBOR, are illustrated for various interest rate scenarios in column five of Table 6.5

By dividing the change in the bank's net interest income resulting from each interest rate scenario by the gain or loss resulting from a $1 million swap under the same interest rate scenario, the notional amount of swaps required to hedge the change in the net interest income can be determined. The result of this analysis is illustrated in the fourth column of Table 6.4. Since no hedge is desired if an increase in interest rates causes net interest income to expand, the column indicates recommended notional swap amounts only for the various declining interest rate scenarios. A notional swap

Table 6.5 Cash Flow of a $1 Million Swap Given Various Interest Rate Scenarios

Rate Change In Basis Points	Fixed Swap Rate Received	90-Day Libor Paid	Net Interest Margin	Net Interest Cash Flow
−400	9.00%	5.00%	+4.00%	+$40,000
−300	9.00%	6.00%	+3.00%	+$30,000
−200	9.00%	7.00%	+2.00%	+$20,000
−100	9.00%	8.00%	+1.00%	+$10,000
–0–	9.00%	9.00%	–0–	–0–
+100	9.00%	10.00%	−1.00%	−$10,000
+200	9.00%	11.00%	−2.00%	−$20,000
+300	9.00%	12.00%	−3.00%	−$30,000
+400	9.00%	13.00%	−4.00%	−$40,000

amount of $55 million is required to hedge the decline in the net interest income up to the point where the basis compression begins to accelerate the deterioration of the net interest income. Table 6.6 illustrates how the $55 million swap reacts under various interest rate scenarios to offset the variance in the bank's net interest income.

It is important to note that the change in the net interest cash flow generated by the swap is $550,000 for each 100 basis point change in interest rates. In other words, the cash flow generated by a swap under various interest rate scenarios is a linear function. However, the change in the bank's net interest margin given the same interest rate scenarios does not change by the same amount and is therefore curvilinear. These relationships are illustrated in Figures 6.4 and 6.5. Although swaps are excellent vehicles to hedge the linear

Table 6.6 Asset-Sensitive Bank Hedged with Interest Rate Swaps

Rate Scenario	Change in the Bank's Net Interest Income	Net Interest Cash Flow of a $55M Swap	Net Variance
−400 Basis Points	−$3,000,000	+$2,200,000	−$800,000
−300	−$2,000,000	+$1,650,000	−$350,000
−200	−$1,100,000	+$1,100,000	–0–
−100	−$ 550,000	+$ 550,000	–0–
–0–	–0–	–0–	–0–
+100	+$ 550,000	−$ 550,000	–0–
+200	+$1,100,000	−$1,100,000	–0–
+300	+$2,000,000	−$1,650,000	+$350,000
+400	+$3,000,000	−$2,200,000	+$800,000

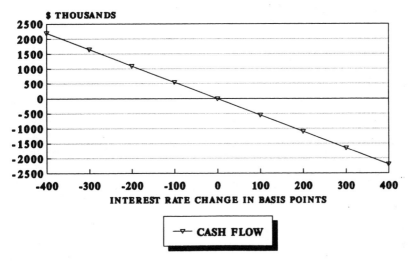

Figure 6.4 Annual cash flow produced by a $55 million swap under various rate scenarios

portion of the variation in a bank's net interest income caused by interest rate changes, they are unable to address the curvilinear risk function that occurs as a result of basis risk.

Options—Caps and Floors

An interest rate cap is an agreement between the seller of the cap and the buyer in which the seller agrees to pay the buyer the difference between the index rate stated in the agreement and the current market rate if the current market rate exceeds the rate stated in the agreement. The amount of the payment is determined by multiplying the rate differential by the notional amount of the agreement. In exchange for

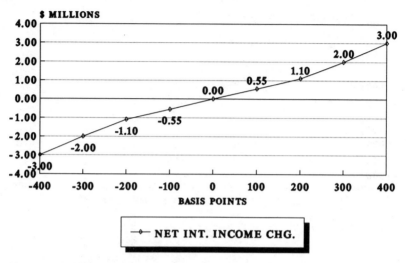

Figure 6.5 Effect of a change in interest rates on a bank's annual net interest income

the opportunity to benefit from a rise in interest rates, the buyer pays the seller a fee at the start of the agreement period. The amount of the fee paid to the provider of the cap is a function of the length of time the cap will be in force, recent market volatility and the relation of the stated cap rate to the current rate. The longer the period of time the cap will be in force, the higher the price of the cap. Cap prices will also be higher during periods of increased volatility in interest rates. When the cap rate is the same as the current rate, the cap is said to be trading at-the-money. If the cap rate is above the current rate, the cap is said to be out-of-the-money. An out-of-the-money cap will sell at a lower price than an at-the-money cap, because interest rates must increase to the level of the cap rate before any money is

Table 6.7 Prime-Rate Caps with a Two-Year Term

Description	Cap Rate (%)	Cap Price (Basis Points)
400 Basis Points Out-of-the-Money	14.00	5
300 Basis Points Out-of-the-Money	13.00	10
200 Basis Points Out-of-the-Money	12.00	20
100 Basis Points Out-of-the-Money	11.00	35
At-the-Money (Current Prime Rate)	10.00	60
100 Basis Points In-the-Money	9.00	160
200 Basis Points In-the-Money	8.00	260
300 Basis Points In-the-Money	7.00	360
400 Basis Points In-the-Money	6.00	460

received by the buyer of the cap, whereas the buyer of an at-the-money cap will begin to receive money when any increase in the interest rate occurs. The highest priced interest rate cap is an in-the-money cap. In this case the cap rate is lower than the current market index rate. Table 6.7 illustrates the pricing structure of two-year prime-rate caps.

Caps are an excellent transaction hedging instrument for loans that have an interest rate ceiling as part of the loan agreement. For example, if a two-year loan is made at prime when the prime lending rate is 10% and contains a rate ceiling of 13%, the bank will generate additional interest income on the loan with any increase in the prime lending rate up to and including 13%. However, if the prime lending rate rises above 13%, the bank's return on the loan will remain at 13% while the cost of funding the loan continues to increase. To hedge this risk, the bank can buy a 13% prime-rate cap. If it was purchased at the time of the loan closing it would be relatively inexpensive because it would be 300 basis points out-of-the-money. If the notional amount of the cap equals the principle amount of the loan, and prime rate increases above 13%, the additional income generated by the cap would offset the fact the loan rate was stopped at 13% (Table 6.8). Before constructing the hedge, the bank must be sure it has sufficient prepayment penalties so the principle of the hedged loan is not reduced during the period of the hedge otherwise the bank may find itself in an overhedged position.

Caps are also useful in constructing balance sheet hedges. Swaps and futures hedge interest rate risk by locking in the current net interest income, whereas caps and floors function more like an insurance policy against interest rate risk. For a onetime up-front fee, a cap or floor will pay benefits to the buyer if a change in interest rates goes against the interest rate risk exposure inherent in the bank's balance sheet structure. If the interest rate change is favorable to the interest rate risk position of the bank's balance sheet, the bank can retain the benefits rather than paying them away as with a swap or futures hedge. That is, a cap or floor does not lock in the existing net interest margin, but allows the bank to benefit from a favorable change in interest rates and insures the bank's net interest income against erosion due to an unfavorable movement in interest rates.

A floor is the opposite of a cap. An interest rate floor is an agreement between the seller of the floor and the buyer, in which the seller agrees to pay the buyer the difference between the index rate stated in the agreement and the current market rate if the current market rate is less than the rate stated in the agreement. For this reason, floors are a valuable hedge against the basis compression, which causes

Table 6.8 $10 Million Floating Prime-Rate Loan with a 13% Rate Limit Hedged by a 13% Cap

Prime Rate Scenario	Annual Income Generated by a $10 Million Prime Based Loan with a 13% Rate Limit	Annual Income Generated by a $10 Million 13% Prime Rate Cap	Annual Cost (1) of a $10 Million 13% Prime Rate Cap	Annual Net Income Generated by the Hedged Loan
14%	1,300,000	100,000	5,000	1,395,000
13%	1,300,000	-0-	5,000	1,295,000
12%	1,200,000	-0-	5,000	1,195,000
11%	1,100,000	-0-	5,000	1,095,000
10% (2)	1,000,000	-0-	5,000	995,000
9%	900,000	-0-	5,000	895,000
8%	800,000	-0-	5,000	795,000
7%	700,000	-0-	5,000	695,000
6%	600,000	-0-	5,000	595,000

1. The cost of a two-year 13% cap is 10 basis points (See Table 6.7). However, the cost is allocated over the term of the cap.
2. Current Prime Lending Rate.

the net interest margin to decline as interest rates move to the lower extremes of their range.

If the asset-sensitive bank described in Table 6.6 had used a notional amount of $55 million at-the-money floors as a hedge, the resulting cash flow would occur as illustrated in Table 6.9. The bank retains most of the income advantage of being asset sensitive in a rising rate environment and hedges most of the decline in the net interest income as interest rates fall. The cost of a three-year term at-the-money prime rate floor is 190 basis points. The $1,045,000 cost of the floor ($55,000,000 × .0190 = $1,045,000) must be paid on the date the floor becomes effective. However, for accounting purposes, the cost is amortized over the three-year term of the floor agreement ($1,045,000 divided by 3 = $348,333). Figure 6.6 illustrates the net cash flow resulting from the $55 million of floor agreements.

In Figure 6.4 the cash flow generated by the swap under various interest rate scenarios is seen to be linear as is the cash flow generated by the floor agreement (Figure 6.6). However, the floor does not generate a cash flow until the market rate of interest moves below the stated rate of the floor agreement. These cash flow characteristics enables swaps used in combination with floors to simulate the curvilinear nature of the net interest income. In the example of the asset-sensitive bank in Table 6.10 the $55 million swap offset the erosion of the bank's net interest income as interest rates began to decline, but did not offset the accelerated decline that occurred as much lower interest rates caused basis compression to occur. The accelerated deterioration of earnings can be hedged by adding a series of out-of-the-money floors (floor agreements with stated rates below the current market rate).

Table 6.9 Asset-Sensitive Bank Hedged with LIBOR Rate Floors

Rate Scenario	Change in the Bank's Net Interest Margin	Net Interest Flow of a $55 Million at-the-Money Floor	Annualized Cost of the Floor	Net Variance
-400 Basis Points	-$3,000,000	+$2,200,000	-$348,333	-$1,148,333
-300 Basis Points	-$2,000,000	+$1,650,000	-$348,333	-$ 698,333
-200 Basis Points	-$1,100,000	+$1,100,000	-$348,333	-$ 348,333
-100 Basis Points	-$ 550,000	+$ 550,000	-$348,333	-$ 348,333
-0-	-0-	-0-	-$348,333	-$ 348,333
+100 Basis Points	+$ 550,000	-0-	-$348,333	+$ 201,667
+200 Basis Points	+$1,100,000	-0-	-$348,333	+$ 751,667
+300 Basis Points	+$2,000,000	-0-	-$348,333	+$1,651,667
+400 Basis Points	+$3,000,000	-0-	-$348,333	+$2,651,667

The net variance column in Table 6.6 indicates the amount of net interest income variation not offset by the swap position. By purchasing out-of-the-money floors to generate a cash flow equal to the net variance during extreme declines in interest rates, it is possible to construct a hedge for the erosion of the net interest income under all the declining interest rate scenarios. By matching the term and index rate of the floors with those of the swap, the basis and maturity risks between the hedge instruments can be eliminated. For this reason, LIBOR-based floors with a three-year term were selected to construct the hedge. The positive effect of combining floors and the swap can be seen by comparing the net variance column of Table 6.6 with the net variance column of Table 6.10.

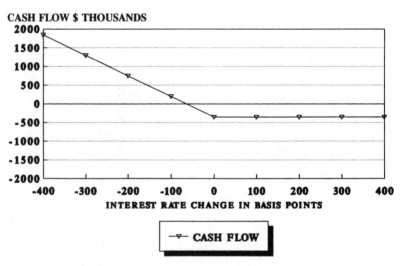

Figure 6.6 Annual cash flow produced by a $55 million floor under various rate scenarios

Table 6.10 Asset-Sensitive Bank Hedged with Interest Rate Swaps and Floors

Rate Scenario[1]	Change in the Bank's Net Interest Margin	Net Interest Flow of a $55 Million Swap	Interest Flows of Various Out-of-the-Money Floors[2]	Annual Cost of Floors	Net Variance
−400 Basis Points	−$3,000,000	+$2,200,000	+$800,000	−$28,167	−$ 28,167
−300 Basis Points	−$2,000,000	+$1,650,000	+$350,000	−$28,167	−$ 28,167
−200 Basis Points	−$1,100,000	+$1,100,000	−0−	−$28,167	−$ 28,167
−100 Basis Points	−$ 550,000	+$ 550,000	−0−	−$28,167	−$ 28,167
−0−	−0−	−0−	−0−	−$28,167	−$ 28,167
+100 Basis Points	+$ 550,000	−$ 550,000	−0−	−$28,167	−$ 28,167
+200 Basis Points	+$1,100,000	−$1,100,000	−0−	−$28,167	−$ 28,167
+300 Basis Points	+$2,000,000	−$1,650,000	−0−	−$28,167	+$321,833
+400 Basis Points	+$3,000,000	−$2,200,000	−0−	−$28,167	+$771,833

1. Current 90-Day Libor Rate is 9%.
2. $35,000,000 Three-Year Floors at 7% were purchased for 21 basis points (Annualized Cost $24,500), and $10,000,000 Three-Year Floors at 6% were purchased for 11 basis points (Annualized Cost $3,667).

Summary

Futures, swaps, caps and floors each possess distinct and very different characteristics. Futures reflect the change in the value of a fixed-income instrument as interest rates change. Therefore, it is better suited to hedge the value of a specific asset or the net asset value of a financial institution than to hedge the changes in net interest income. Interest rate swaps are a more appropriate hedge for variations in net interest income caused by a change in interest rates. However, A/L managers must remember a swap hedges by locking in the existing net interest income. What is gained when interest rates move in favor of the bank's interest rate risk position is given up by the interest rate swap hedge. Caps and floors hedge by protecting the net interest margin, much like an insurance policy. It protects the financial institution from changes in interest rates that would cause the net interest income to decline, yet it allows the institution to benefit from favorable changes in interest rates. The price of retaining the advantages of a favorable change in interest rates is a premium that can, at times, be quite substantial.

Brokerage firms and investment bankers offer a bewildering array of swaps, caps, and floors. This occurs because these instruments are basically agreements between two parties, and can be constructed to conform to the requirements of both parties. For example, there are delayed start swaps that do not take effect until some future date, there are basis swaps that exchange two floating interest rates such as prime and 90-day LIBOR, and there are caps and floors based on the prime rate as well as LIBOR. If there are no synthetic instruments available to hedge a bank's particular balance sheet position, one can probably be created. It is important to develop a good working relationship with investment banks and brokerage firms. Once their professional staff becomes aware of the bank's specific balance sheet hedging requirements, they can either find the appropriate instrument or create one.

The A/L manager must always remember that the bank's balance sheet structure, customer base, operating environment and management style make their bank unique from all the other banks. If the bank's A/L managers have conducted a thorough analysis of the bank and carefully modeled the bank using one of the excellent A/L management software models now available in the marketplace, no one on Wall Street will know their bank as well as they do. Examined in isolation, a synthetic hedging instrument may appear to meet the bank's hedging needs; however, its interaction with all the elements comprising the bank's balance sheet must be explored before the instrument can be deemed to be an appropriate hedge. This is why it is critically important to model-test the various hedges recommended by outside consultants. The model testing should include various time horizons, such as twelve months and five years, various interest rate scenarios, including changes in basis relationships and yield curve shapes as well as changes in the overall level of interest rates, and various embedded option scenarios, such as changes in the prepayment speed of the mortgages. The A/L manager must be very knowledgeable about the synthetic instrument and completely aware of its impact on the bank's financial performance under various possible scenarios.

Once the most appropriate hedge has been determined, the A/L manager must provide the information to the ALCO. It is critically important for the members of the

ALCO to thoroughly understand why a hedge is being suggested, be familiar with the recommended synthetic hedging instrument, and be aware of its financial impact on the bank under various interest rate scenarios and changes in the balance sheet structure. Synthetic instruments can be extremely effective in managing a bank's interest rate risk exposure, but because they can very quickly cause a major shift in a bank's interest rate risk position, they must be used very carefully.

7

Interest Rate Forecasting

Most bankers say it is impossible to forecast interest rates, while others say it is possible to forecast the general direction of rate movements for short periods of time. In spite of this ambivalence, the fact remains that the rate forecast embedded in a bank's balance sheet structure extends many years into the future.

Every balance sheet is a forecast about the future direction of interest rates. If a bank is using a disproportionately large amount of short-term liabilities to fund long-term fixed-rate assets, the balance sheet is structured to benefit from a decline in interest rates. The balance sheet forecast may or may not be congruous with management's interest rate forecast. If interest rates are expected to move sharply higher, long-term fixed-rate assets should not be funded with short-term liabilities. The primary job of the asset/liability manager is to determine the interest rate forecast embedded in the bank's balance sheet and adjust it to be compatible with senior management's interest rate forecast.

The easiest way to identify the rate forecast embedded in the balance sheet is to use an asset/liability management simulation model. If a rising rate scenario is used in the model and the net interest income increases, the balance sheet has been structured to benefit from rising rates. On the other hand, if a declining rate scenario produces a larger net interest income, the balance sheet has been structured to benefit from declining rates.

Other chapters of this book deal with determining the interest rate forecast defined by the balance sheet structure, and adjusting it to management's rate forecast. This chapter will focus on the process by which the senior managers develop their interest rate forecast. Forecasting interest rates is precarious. Senior bank executives have never been able to consistently predict with a high degree of accuracy the direction of interest rate movements let alone reliably forecast the magnitude and timing of interest rate changes. Nevertheless, if senior bank executives are going to manage their bank effectively, they must take a position on the direction, magnitude, and timing of future interest rate movements.

THE EXPECTATION THEORY OF FORECASTING INTEREST RATES

The expectation theory for the term structure of interest rates defines the yield curve as the collective interest rate forecast of all the participants in the fixed income markets. As the market participants' collective rate forecast changes, so does the shape and level of the yield curve. It also states that the current long-term rate of interest is equal to the average of the series of short-term interest rates expected to occur during the long-term period. In essence, the long-term rate is the average of the present and future short-term rates.

According to this theory, future interest rate movements can be determined by the shape of the current yield curve. For example, if the yield curve is inverted (i.e., current short-term interest rates are higher than current long-term interest rates) a decline in interest rates is anticipated. The theory states the decline in short-term interest rates will occur because the current long-term interest rate is lower than the current short-term interest rates, therefore the future short-term interest rates must be lower than the current short-term interest rate because the current long-term rate is the average of the present and future short-term

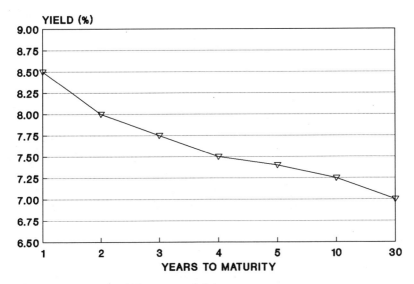

Figure 7.1 Inverted Treasury yield curve

rates. Figure 7.1 illustrates an inverted yield curve. Using the current one-year Treasury rate of 8.5% and the current two-year Treasury rate of 8%, the equation in Table 7.1 forecasts the one-year Treasury rate, one year from now at 7.5%.[1]

Table 7.1 Implied Forward Interest Rate Forecast with Inverted Yield Curve

Current One-Year Treasury Bill Rate	= 8.50%
Current Two-Year Treasury Note Rate	= 8.00%
One-Year Treasury Bill Rate One Year From Now	= X
Number of Years In the Analysis Period	= 2
The Future One-Year Treasury Bill Rate	$= \dfrac{8.5 + X}{2} = 8$
	$X = 7.50\%$

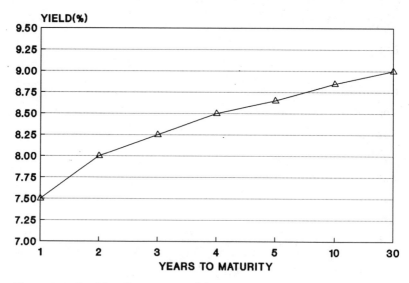

Figure 7.2 Positive Treasury yield curve

On the other hand, if the yield curve has a positive slope (current short-term rates are lower than current long-term rates) an increase in interest rates is anticipated. Figure 7.2 illustrates a positively sloped yield curve. If the current one-year Treasury rate is 7.5%, and the current two-year Treasury rate is 8%, it may be concluded that the one-year Treasury rate, one year from now, will be 8.5%. The computation of this future rate is illustrated in Table 7.2.

The yield curve also provides information about the magnitude and timing of the expected interest rate movements. If the yield curve is sharply inverted, a dramatic decline in interest rates is expected. Whereas a very positively sloped yield curve indicates the market anticipates a signifi-

Table 7.2 Implied Forward Interest Rate Forecast with Positive Yield Curve

Current One-Year Treasury Bill Rate	= 7.50%
Current Two-Year Treasury Note Rate	= 8.00%
One-Year Treasury Bill Rate One Year From Now	= X
Number of Years In the Analysis Period	= 2
The Future One-Year Treasury Bill Rate	$= \dfrac{7.5 + X}{2} = 8$
	$X = 8.50\%$

cant increase in interest rates. The humped yield curve, illustrated in Figure 7.3 indicates that the market anticipates interest rates to rise for two years, then decline gradually over the remaining years.

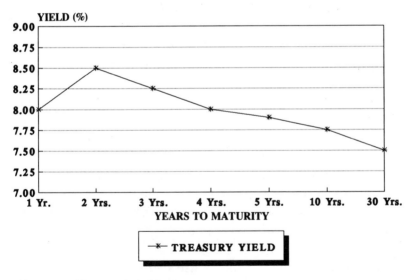

Figure 7.3 Humped yield curve

When using this theory to forecast interest rates, it is important to remember two points. First, investors generally demand a risk premium to encourage them to purchase longer maturities.[2] The yield curve will, therefore, have a slightly positive slope even when the collective market forecast is for interest rates to remain unchanged. Second, this method of forecasting interest rates has often failed to correctly predict rate movements because the participants in the fixed income markets did not correctly anticipate changes in the rate of inflation or in the level of economic activity.[3] Nevertheless, it is of value to the A/L manager because it provides a way to determine the market's collective interest rate forecast.

CONSULTING OUTSIDE ECONOMISTS

Interest rates result from the complex relationships between various elements of the economy, such as the supply of money, the demand for credit, the rate of inflation, the level of economic activity, and the interest rates offered in other countries. A change in any of these factors may cause a major shift in interest rates. The interest rate forecast, resulting from the expectation theory, is based on the market's collective wisdom. However, the markets often incorrectly anticipate certain changes in the major elements of the economy. To compensate for this problem an A/L manager will often consult with an economist.

Most of the large banks have an economist on staff, however, many smaller banks use economists from outside their institution, not only to provide a rate forecast, but also to explain the anticipated changes in the economic environment. It is important for the senior management to understand the reasoning behind the interest rate forecast in order to compare and contrast various forecasts. A source of useful information is financial newspapers, such as the *Wall Street Journal* and *Barrons*. These newspapers frequently feature articles by or interviews with leading economists in which they explain their view of the economic environment and their interest rate forecasts. Twice a year, the *Wall Street Journal* lists the names of the leading economists and their firms, measures the accuracy of their last six-month forecasts, and presents their forecasts for the next six months. Other sources of information about the economy are television programs, such as Wall Street Week and the Nightly Business Report and the Financial News Network. To directly consult with a leading economist, an arrangement can usually be made with most brokerage houses or correspondent banks to meet with their economists. If a particular economist in whom an A/L manager is interested is employed by a consulting firm, the bank must pay a consulting fee for access to the economist.

USING PAST HISTORY

Another way to measure a bank's potential risk exposure to a change in interest rates is to examine the extremes to which interest rates have moved during the past few business cycles. By using sources such as back issues of the *Wall Street Journal* or old *Federal Reserve Bulletins*, it is possible to determine not only the highest and lowest levels reached by interest rates during past business cycles, but also the steepest positive and negative slopes of the yield curve.

Table 7.3 The Extremes Which Treasury Interest Rates
Have Moved Since 1985 (January 1, 1985–March 31, 1992)

Term	Lowest Treasury Rates 1/08/92	Highest Treasury Rates 3/31/89	Steepest Negative Yield Curve 7/28/89	Steepest Positive Yield Curve 3/05/92
3 Month	3.81%	9.18%	8.10%	4.13%
6 Month	3.89	9.50	7.89	4.29
1 Year	3.98	9.59	7.67	4.56
2 Year	4.62	9.66	7.54	5.58
3 Year	4.94	9.58	7.60	6.04
5 Year	5.91	9.47	7.58	6.84
7 Year	6.40	9.36	7.71	7.14
10 Year	6.75	9.27	7.85	7.47
30 Year	7.39	9.09	7.98	7.93

Each of these extremes can be used as an interest rate scenario in the bank's asset/liability simulation model. If a particular scenario produces a compression in net interest income that is unacceptable to senior management, the asset/liability management committee should consider taking action to reduce the negative impact. The extremes to which interest rates moved from 1985 through March of 1992 are illustrated in Table 7.3 and Figure 7.4.

To develop a worse-case scenario based on recent history, a yield curve can be constructed using the highest level reached by 30-year Treasury bond rates during the past cycle as a starting point, then construct a yield curve based on the steepest yield curve inversion of the past business cycle. The opposite worst-case scenario could be constructed using the lowest 90-day Treasury bill yield of the last business cycle

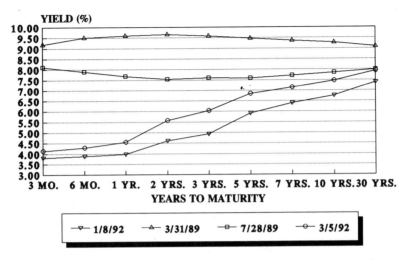

Figure 7.4 The extremes to which Treasury interest rates have moved (January 1, 1985–March 31, 1992)

and the steepest positive slope of the yield curve realized during that cycle.

The recent history of interest rates can also be extremely useful when modeling basis risk. Many asset/liability models use the Treasury yield curve as the basis for all rates used in the model. Therefore, it is important to understand the variation in the spreads between the deposit, loan, and investment rates, and the equivalent maturity Treasury rate.

Figure 7.5 illustrates the wide swings that have occurred in interest rates since 1985. As one-year Treasury bill rates moved from 10% down to 5.5%, then back to over 9.5% before beginning another descent, the net interest margin of banks with a severely mismatched gap position would have compressed and expanded in an accordionlike fashion. Also,

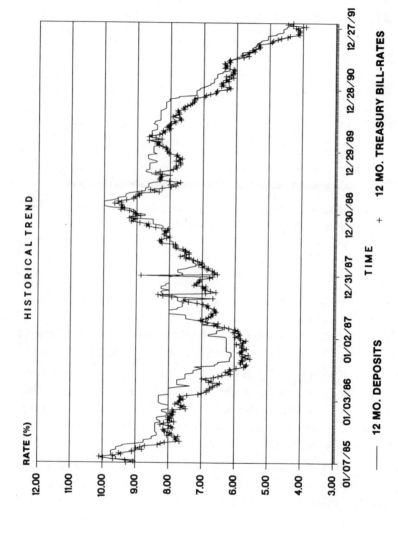

Figure 7.5 12 mo. deposit rates and 12 mo. Treasury bill-rates

embedded in these rate swings is a more subtle risk, that of basis risk. In addition to the one-year Treasury bill rate, the one-year regional bank deposit rates have been included in Figure 7.5. At first glance it appears the one-year deposit rate moves roughly in tandem with the one-year Treasury rate. However, on closer inspection it is observed that sometimes the deposit rate is 40 basis points below the Treasury rate, while at other times it is 140 basis points above the Treasury rate (Figure 7.6). Therefore, in addition to the risk generated by the absolute movement of interest rates during the business cycle, there also exists a basis risk that in this example could cause a variation in the net interest margin of 180 basis points. To fully understand a bank's exposure to movements in interest rates, the basis risk must be considered. It is essential to include an estimate of the change in the basis relationships when developing an interest rate forecast.

Each bank has its own unique exposure to basis risk. It is as individual as a fingerprint. This occurs because each city and region has its own competitive environment. Also, each banks' management has its individual philosophy regarding how aggressive to be when pricing deposits and loans. Measuring basis risk by using market rates and national averages will not produce the accuracy that is possible if each A/L manager takes the time to compute their bank's basis risk.

To measure a bank's basis risk, the A/L manager must collect information as to the rates that were paid on the bank's various deposit accounts and loans over a period of time long enough to encompass numerous changes in interest rates and the shape of the yield curve. An appropriate period is usually the span of one business cycle. Meanwhile, the

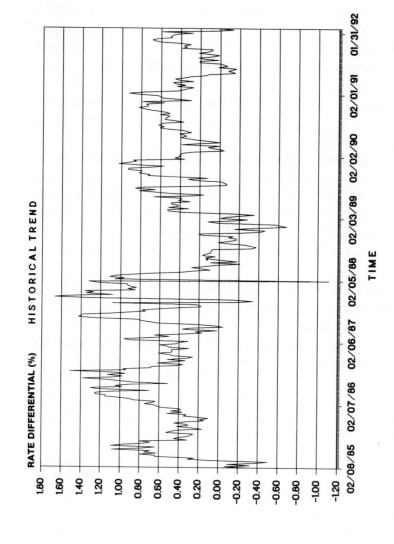

Figure 7.6 12 mo. deposit rates minus 12 mo. Treasury bill-rates

bank must collect information as to various Treasury rates with maturities equivalent to those of the various time deposits and loans during the same period. For example, 12-month Treasury bill rates covering a period of 87 months can be compared with 12-month deposit rates during the same period. By subtracting the Treasury rates from the deposit rates, the degree of variation in basis will be revealed (Table 7.4). To enable the bank's management to forecast the change in the basis relationship and thus be able to include it when using the A/L modeling system, it is necessary to divide the 12-month Treasury bill into its various component levels. This is illustrated in Table 7.5 in the column entitled "range". This exercise reveals that the cost of a one-year time deposit is significantly above the Treasury rate when Treasury rates are low. However, as Treasury rates move higher, the cost of a 12-month time deposit versus a 12-month Treasury bill becomes progressively less until it finally becomes negative as the Treasury bill rises above 10%. Therefore, if the interest rate forecast predicts one-year Treasury bills to be between 7.01% and 7.50%, it can be anticipated that the cost of one-year time deposits will be approximately 47 basis points greater than the underlying one-year Treasury bill rate. If the forecast is for rates to decline below 7%, it can be anticipated that the cost of one-year time deposits will increase relative to the Treasury bill rate. If the forecast is for a rise in interest rates above 7.5%, it can be anticipated that the cost of funding a 12-month time deposit will decline relative to the underlying yield of a one-year Treasury bill. This example is especially pertinent because many banks have a one-year adjustable-rate mortgage portfolio that is primarily funded by 12-month time deposits. From a gap standpoint this is a perfect match

Table 7.4 Twelve Month Deposit Rates Minus Twelve Month Treasury Bill Rates (Excerpt from study encompassing January 1, 1985–March 31, 1992)

Range: 7.51–8.00			12 Mo. Dep. Minus	
Date	12 Month Dep.	12 Month T-Rates	12 Mo. T-Rates	
05/27/88	7.50	7.68	−0.18	
06/03/88	7.50	7.55	−0.05	
06/24/88	7.55	7.51	0.04	
07/01/88	7.70	7.53	0.17	
07/08/88	7.75	7.60	0.15	
07/15/88	7.90	7.81	0.09	
07/22/88	7.90	7.81	0.09	
07/29/88	7.90	7.82	0.08	
08/05/88	7.90	7.83	0.07	
09/16/88	8.00	7.99	0.01	
07/07/89	8.65	7.97	0.68	
07/14/89	8.65	7.83	0.82	
07/21/89	8.65	8.00	0.65	
07/28/89	8.65	7.79	0.86	
08/04/89	8.50	7.69	0.81	
09/15/89	8.25	8.00	0.25	
10/13/89	8.73	8.00	0.73	
10/20/89	8.62	7.91	0.71	
10/27/89	8.62	7.80	0.82	
11/03/89	8.62	7.82	0.80	
11/10/89	8.62	7.83	0.79	
11/17/89	8.62	7.69	0.93	
11/24/89	8.62	7.69	0.93	
12/01/89	8.40	7.70	0.70	Results of the
12/05/89	8.40	7.83	0.57	Complete Study
				Average 0.45
				Std. Dev. 0.32
				Variance 0.10
				Minimum −0.21
				Maximum 1.09

Table 7.5 Basis Relationship of 12 Month Time Deposits
vs. 12 Month Treasury Bills

Range (%)	Average (%)	Minimum (%)	Maximum (%)
5.51–6.00	0.59	0.26	1.51
6.01–6.50	0.90	0.17	1.38
6.51–7.00	0.95	−0.04	1.67
7.01–7.50	0.47	0.03	0.93
7.51–8.00	0.45	−0.21	1.09
8.01–8.50	0.13	−0.37	1.08
8.51–9.00	0.11	−1.11	0.80
9.01–9.50	0.07	−0.68	0.64
9.51–10.00	0.01	−0.50	0.42
10.01–10.50	−0.50	−0.50	0.00

and there is no apparent interest rate risk. However, when basis risk is taken into consideration, it can be seen that the average net interest margin on this particular arbitrage can vary by as much as 145 basis points. By conducting this analysis for each of the various categories of deposits and loans, the bank's basis risk can be measured and incorporated in the A/L modeling process.

If a bank is to effectively manage its net interest margin, it must go through this exercise. Outside economists and general forecasts of interest rates cannot fully anticipate the extent to which an individual bank is exposed to basis risk. Every bank's interest rate forecast should include anticipated changes in basis relationships.

SUMMARY

A well-managed bank will have a balance sheet structure that produces a satisfactory level of net interest income if the bank's interest rate forecast is correct, yet it will not be devastated should a realistic worse-case scenario come to pass. The bank's interest rate forecast should be the product of yield curve analysis, economists' forecasts, and an analysis of the recent history of interest rate movements. Using these sources, bank management can establish the realistic extremes to which interest rates could move during the remainder of the business cycle, and an estimate can be produced as to the most likely movement of interest rates during the period. The forecasts should include changes in the basis relationships between the various interest rates of Treasury securities and the major balance sheet components as well as changes in the general level of interest rates and the shape of the yield curve. These forecasts should then be entered into the simulation model to see what effect each scenario will have on the bank's net interest income. The most likely interest rate forecast should produce a net interest income that meets the bank's profit objectives. Also, the two extreme forecasts should not have a disastrous impact on the net interest income. If a satisfactory return is not produced by the most likely interest rate forecast or a disastrous impact on the net interest income occurs because of the extreme forecasts, management must take action to reduce the institution's interest rate risk.

1. This equation does not take into account the effect of compounding during the long period of time represented by the yield curve. For a detailed discussion of the actual computation of the implied forward rates, see Charles P. Jones, *Investments Analysis and Managment*, New York, Wiley, 1985, pp. 193–197.

2. R. Ibbatson and R. Sinquefield, *Stocks, Bonds, Bills and Inflation: The Past And The Future*, 1982 ed., Monograph no. 15. Charlottesville, VA: The Financial Analysis Research Foundation, University of Virginia, 1982.

3. Charles P. Jones, *Investments Analysis and Management*, New York, Wiley, 1985, p. 197.

8

Conducting a Self-Analysis

An effective asset/liability committee (ALCO) must be dedicated to knowing the true financial condition of the bank. To accomplish this, the A/L manager must conduct a thorough analysis of the bank and present the findings to the ALCO. The committee's responsibility is to be open to new ideas, which at times might challenge some of the closely held concepts of various members of the committee. The discussions that occur during the process of self-examination frequently produce insights that result in excellent A/L management strategies. Therefore, it is essential that the ALCO not be a rubber-stamp committee controlled by one dominant personality. An effective ALCO is an open forum where the free flow of information and ideas result in actions that enhance the bank's ability to attain its goals and objectives.

There are five basic areas to be explored when conducting an analysis of any financial institution. They are: earnings, liquidity, capital adequacy, asset quality, and interest rate risk exposure. The A/L manager is directly responsible for managing the bank's interest rate risk exposure, providing adequate liquidity, and producing a satisfactory level of net interest income. Although A/L managers spend a great deal of time conducting in-depth analyses of these areas, they must also monitor the bank's capital position, asset quality, and various components of the bank's net income other than the net interest income. The A/L manager must present the information to the ALCO members to provide them with a comprehensive understanding of the bank's exposure to risks. Their decisions can have a major impact on many areas of the bank, so they must be kept well informed.

Each of the areas are analyzed from three different vantage points: static, dynamic, and peer group comparisons.

The static analysis uses the information contained in the bank's most recent financial statement to analyze the bank's financial condition. In addition to analyzing the bank's current condition, static analysis identifies the statistics and ratios that will be used for the dynamic analysis and peer group comparisons.

The major problem with a static analysis is its failure to reflect trends occurring within the bank. By combining a series of static analyses from various periods, a dynamic analysis is created in which trends can be identified. For example, the static analysis may show a bank's loan to deposit ratio is 85%. Although this ratio may be within the bank's policy limit of 90%, a dynamic analysis might indicate the ratio was 80% last year and 75% the year before that. If this trend continues, the bank could soon violate its policy limit of 90%. The ALCO must be aware of the trend, investigate the cause, and take corrective action before it becomes a problem.

A dynamic analysis will provide a great deal of information about the financial condition and trends within an individual bank. However, it will not indicate to what extent the environment within which the bank must operate is responsible for producing the condition or trends. Only by comparing the bank's static and dynamic analysis with those of similar financial institutions operating in the same market area can the ALCO determine whether a particular trend is unique to their bank. If the trend is unique to the bank, very likely the cause of the trend is the manner in which the bank is being managed. To reverse the trend, the bank need only change some of its management strategies or policies. If the trend is also occurring in numerous other banks in the area, there is usually a factor in the banking environment that is causing the trend. The bank cannot control the environment, so management must implement strategies to alter the bank's performance to counter the trend. Peer group information for various types of financial institutions delineated by asset size and geographic location can be obtained from the Federal Reserve Bank, state banking associations, and private consulting firms such as the Thomson BankWatch Service; Sheshunoff; Lyons, Zomback, and Ostrowski, Inc. and Keefe, Bruyette and Woods.

PROFIT ANALYSIS

The primary purpose for creating a financial institution is to produce a profit. The profit is the amount of dollars remaining after the bank has deducted its expenses from its total income and is reported on the income statement as net income. Net income by itself is a very basic measure of how well the bank's management has done in profitably managing the bank. It indicates only that a bank has either made or lost money. Net income provides no detailed information about how skillfully the bank's management has utilized the bank's capital, deployed its assets, and managed its expenses. To determine this information, bank analysts compute the return on average equity (net income divided by average equity) and the return on average total assets (net income divided by average total assets).

Management is ultimately responsible to the shareholders because they are the owners of the bank's capital. The return on average equity (ROE) is important because it indicates how well the management has employed the bank's capital. If the ROE was 6% last year when one-year Treasury bills produced an 8% return, the bank's management team did not do a satisfactory job of employing the capital. The shareholders could have earned 2% more if the bank had been liquidated and the proceeds placed in Treasury bills. An ROE must be substantially above the one-year Treasury bill rate to be regarded as a satisfactory return. For example, if management can generate an ROE in excess of 10% during a time when the one-year Treasury bill rate is 8%, it would be considered as doing an adequate job of managing the shareholders' capital. The banking business entails considerably more risk than simply owning a Treasury instrument and shareholders must be compensated for the additional risk.

The major problem with focusing on ROE as the primary measurement of a bank's profitability is that it does not take into consideration the leverage factor. A bank can greatly increase its ROE by heavily leveraging itself. That is, it can use its equity to support a very large amount of assets. For example, if a $100 million bank earned a 1% return on average total assets (ROA) it would produce a net income of $1 million each year. If it had $25 million in capital, its leverage ratio (average total assets divided by average equity) would be four and its ROE would be 4% (net income divided by average equity). Although the bank earned $1 million, it is a very poor return on the shareholders' capital. If it could expand its assets to $300 million while continuing to earn 1% ROA it would produce $3 million of net income and its ROE would be 12% ($3 million divided by $25 million). With asset levels of $600 million, the bank's ROE would be 24%, at $1.2 billion, the ROE would be 48% and its leverage ratio would be 48. ($1.2 Billion divided by $25 million)

It is dangerous for management to focus solely on ROE as a measure of the bank's profitability because it encourages highly leveraged positions. A highly leveraged position is a wonderful thing as long as all is going well. However, a relatively minor difficulty can be magnified into a major problem for a highly leveraged institution. To limit the degree to which banks can leverage their capital as they attempt to improve their ROE, bank regulators have established minimum capital to risk asset ratios that must be maintained.

A better assessment of a bank's profitability can be obtained from the ROA. The ROA reflects how effectively the bank's management team is employing the assets and cannot be skewed by increased leverage. The problem with focusing primarily on the ROA occurs when a bank is grossly underleveraged. It may have a good ROA, but its very conservative leverage position produces a very low ROE. To understand how effectively a bank is being managed in regard to generating profits, an analyst must look at ROE and ROA and balance the two with an assessment of the risk inherent in the bank's leveraged position.

It is very beneficial to separate ROA into its various components in order to gain an understanding of how a particular bank generates profits. The major component of a bank's profit is the net interest income. Since the ALCO is primarily responsible for managing the net interest income, it is useful to thoroughly examine the net interest income by reducing it into its basic elements. By understanding profits in this manner, an analyst can isolate the elements within the bank that are causing an adverse trend in ROE or ROA. The analytic structure frequently used to conduct the analysis is referred to as the Dupont Earnings Analysis. The structure of the analysis is presented in Figure 8.1. The title inside each box identifies the interest rate or ratio to be used in the

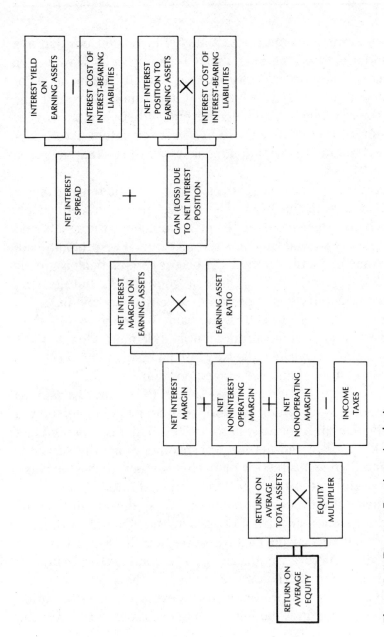

Figure 8.1 Dupont Earnings Analysis

Table 8.1 Explanation of Ratios Used in the Dupont Earnings Analysis

Return on Average Equity = Net Income After Tax ÷ Average Equity

Return on Average Total Assets = Net Income After Tax ÷ Average Total Assets

Equity Multiplier = Average Total Assets ÷ Average Equity

Net Interest Margin = (Total Interest Income − Total Interest Expense) ÷ Average Total Assets

Net Noninterest Operating Margin = (Noninterest Operating Income − Noninterest Operating Expenses) ÷ Average Total Assets

Net Nonoperating Margin = (Nonoperating Income − Nonoperating Expense) ÷ Average Total Assets

Income Taxes = Income Tax Paid ÷ Average Total Assets

Net Interest Margin on Earning Assets = (Total Interest Income − Total Interest Expense) ÷ Average Earning Assets

Earning Asset Ratio = Average Earning Assets ÷ Average Total Assets

Net Interest Spread = Interest Yield on Earning Assets − Interest Cost of Interest-Bearing Liabilities

Gain (Loss) Due to Net Interest Position = Net Interest Position to Earning Assets × Interest Cost of Interest-Bearing Liabilities

Interest Yield on Earning Assets = Total Interest Income ÷ Average Earning Assets

Interest Cost of Interest-Bearing Liabilities = Total Interest Expense ÷ Average Interest-Bearing Liabilities

Net Interest Position to Earning Assets = (Average Earning Assets − Average Interest-Bearing Liabilities) ÷ Average Earning Assets

analysis. Table 8.1 lists and explains each of the titles. Between some of the boxes are mathematic symbols indicating the operation to be performed. For example, the upper-right side of the model illustrates that by subtracting the

185

interest cost of interest-bearing liabilities from the interest yield on earning assets, the net interest spread is produced. Adding the gain or loss due to the net interest position to the net interest spread creates the net interest margin on earning assets. Multiplying the net interest margin on earning assets by the earning asset ratio results in the net interest margin. The model concludes with the derivation of ROA and ROE.

To operate the model thirteen items of data are required that can be obtained from the annual reports or call reports of most financial institutions. The thirteen data elements are listed in Table 8.2. It is important to note all balance sheet

Table 8.2 Data Items Required to Operate the Dupont Earnings Analysis

First National Bank Data ($ Million)			
Item	1988	1989	1990
Average Total Assets	$100.00	$123.75	$156.65
Average Earning Assets	95.47	118.34	149.64
Average Interest-Bearing Liabilities	83.84	104.38	132.36
Average Equity	10.00	11.00	12.05
Total Interest Income	9.47	12.70	15.17
Total Interest Expense	5.68	7.89	9.27
Net Income Before Tax	1.49	1.61	2.04
Income Tax Paid	.49	.56	.91
Net Income After Tax	1.00	1.05	1.13
Noninterest Operating Income	1.00	1.20	1.50
Noninterest Operating Expense	3.41	4.26	5.82
Nonoperating Income	.61	.25	.90
Nonoperating Expense	.50	.40	.45

items are averages. The period of time used as a basis for the averages is the same as the period of time encompassed by the income statement. If 1990 earnings are being analyzed, the balance sheet items will be the average balances for 1990, not the amount reported at year-end 1990.

To demonstrate how effectively the Dupont Earnings Analysis can be used to identify and explain trends in the ROE and ROA, an example has been constructed using the data from the hypothetical First National Bank. The data for the years 1988, 1989, and 1990 are presented in Table 8.2. A visual inspection of the data indicates the bank has experienced rapid growth during the three-year period and is making a profit. However, to go beyond this basic observation requires the use of the Dupont Earnings Analysis model.

The First National Bank data have been processed using the formulas in Table 8.1, the results of which are presented in Figure 8.2. The ROE at 9.36% appears to be a satisfactory return on the Bank's equity: however, the ROE has been steadily eroding during the past three years. The decline was not caused by a reduction in the Bank's leverage position. The increase in the Bank's equity multiplier from 10 in 1988 to 13 in 1990 would have caused an increase in the ROE if the ROA had remained constant. In fact, the ROA has suffered a sharp decline that was masked in part by the increase in the equity multiplier.

To understand the reason for the 28 basis point decline in the Bank's ROA, during the three year period 1988 through 1990 the four components of the ROA must be closely examined. The slight decline in the Bank's net interest margin contributed only 2 basis points to the 28 basis point decline in the ROA (3.79% − 3.77% = .02%). This is an important ratio because the trend in the net interest margin

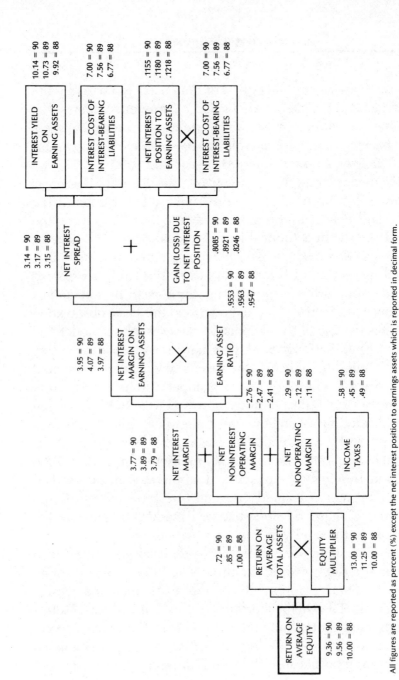

Figure 8.2 Dupont Earnings Analysis—First National Bank

All figures are reported as percent (%) except the net interest position to earnings assets which is reported in decimal form.

is a good test of the ALCO's effectiveness. In this example, the A/L management team did an excellent job of keeping the net interest margin relatively stable during a period when the yield on earning assets went from 9.92% in 1988 to 10.73% in 1989 before settling back to 10.14% in 1990. The analysis reveals the primary cause of the Bank's decline in its ROA to be a rapid increase in its operating expenses. From 1988 through 1990, the rising trend in operating expenses relative to operating revenue caused an erosion of 35 basis points in the bank's net noninterest operating margin (2.41% − 2.76% = − .35%). Security gains realized in 1990 offset much of the increase in operating expenses by causing the net nonoperating margin to contribute 29 basis points to the 1990 ROA. Unless the rising operating costs are deliberately being incurred to support a long-term growth objective, management should quickly implement an expense control program.

Another useful piece of information provided by the analysis is the fact that the net interest margin on earning assets was greatly enhanced by the Bank's positive net interest position. Average earning assets in 1990 totaled $149.64 million while average interest-bearing liabilities totaled $132.36 million; therefore, $17.28 million of interest-bearing assets were funded by liabilities, such as demand deposits and retained earnings on which no interest was paid. When the amount of interest-bearing assets is greater than the amount of interest-bearing liabilities, a financial institution is said to have a positive net interest position. When the reverse is true, a financial institution is said to have a negative net interest position. In 1990 the Bank's positive net interest position provided 80.85 basis points to the net interest margin (.1155 × 7.00 = .8085). If it were not for the positive net interest position, the Bank's ROA and ROE would be completely eliminated. For this reason, the bank should include as part of its planning process strategies and policies that will maintain or improve the net interest position.

Additional insight can be obtained by comparing various ratios with the same ratios produced by other financial institutions during the same time period. If the average net noninterest operating margin for banks in the First National Bank's peer group was −2.45% for the years 1988, 1989, and 1990, the net noninterest operating margin at the First National Bank was about average in 1988 and 1989 and has deteriorated relative to the peer group average in 1990. To increase its net noninterest operating margin to levels significantly above the industry norm would require extraordinary effort. However, the ratio is now significantly below the industry norm so management can bring the ratio in line with its peers by simply realizing average performance.

The Dupont Earnings Analysis is an excellent way to quickly reduce a financial institution's income into its component parts, identify earnings trends, and isolate problem areas. However, the analysis does not address the issues of capital adequacy, asset quality, interest rate risk exposure, or the institution's liquidity position. To analyze these areas other methods of analysis must be employed.

LIQUIDITY ANALYSIS

A financial institution must be able to provide cash to meet customers' demands to withdraw their funds and to service its debt obligations. To be considered as available liquidity, the funds must be provided in a timely manner without generating a significant capital loss. The moment it is unable to meet the depositors' or creditors' demands, the institution has technically failed. This is the minimum amount of liquidity that must be available if a financial institution is to continue to function, and is referred to as essential liquidity.

Most financial institutions go beyond essential liquidity when establishing liquidity objectives. They expand the concept of the institution's liquidity requirement to include providing cash to fund loan demand. This expanded concept of liquidity is referred to as adequate liquidity. A financial institution may have enough liquidity to meet its essential liquidity needs, but if it does not have enough liquidity to fund its customers' loan requests, not only will the institution miss an opportunity to employ funds at an attractive yield, but it could lose the entire customer relationship to another institution that is able to fund the loan request. To meet income and growth objectives, it is necessary for management to go beyond essential liquidity and establish objectives for providing adequate liquidity.

How much liquidity is required to provide adequate liquidity? To answer this question, the requirement for liquidity must be separated into its three major components: short-term requirements, seasonal requirements, and structural requirements. Short-term liquidity requirements arise from the mostly unpredictable day-to-day changes in deposit and loan balances. Although the daily fluctuations in deposits and loans are difficult to predict, management can establish ample reserves to meet these liquidity demands by examining the institution's recent history of daily deposit and loan changes. With the aid of a computer, the daily changes in the deposits are analyzed to determine the largest single daily,

Table 8.3 Analysis of Seasonal Liquidity Requirements

Date	Total Deposits*	Monthly $ Change*	% of Prior Year's Average	Total Loans*	Monthly $ Change*	% of Prior Year's Average
1987 Average	192	N/A	N/A	155	N/A	N/A
January 1988	199	−2	1.036	160	−1	1.032
February	195	−4**	1.016	159	−1	1.026
March	196	+1	1.021	159	−0−	1.026
April	194	−2	1.010	161	+2	1.039
May	199	+5	1.036	163	+2	1.052
June	207	+8	1.078	165	+2	1.065
July	211	+4	1.099	164	−1	1.058
August	213	+2	1.109	163	−1	1.052
September	214	+1	1.115	165	+2	1.065
October	216	+2	1.125	168	+3	1.084
November	218	+2	1.135	169	+1	1.090
December	217	−1	1.130	167	−2	1.077
1988 Average	207	N/A	N/A	164	N/A	N/A
January 1989	214	−3	1.034	166	−1	1.012
February	212	−2	1.024	165	−1	1.006
March	211	−1	1.019	163	−2	.994
April	210	−1	1.014	164	+1	1.000
May	216	+6	1.043	165	+1	1.006

June	219	+3	1.058	167	+2	1.018
July	220	+1	1.063	167	-0-	1.018
August	222	+2	1.072	166	-1	1.012
September	221	-1	1.068	170	+4***	1.037
October	223	+2	1.077	174	+4***	1.061
November	224	+1	1.082	175	+1	1.067
December	225	+1	1.087	176	+1	1.067
1989 Average	218	N/A	N/A	168	N/A	N/A
January 1990	221	-4**	1.034	175	-1	1.042
February	218	-3	1.000	173	-2	1.030
March	216	-2	.991	172	-1	1.024
April	213	-3	.977	174	+2	1.036
May	218	+5	1.000	177	+3	1.054
June	221	+3	1.014	179	+2	1.065
July	224	+3	1.028	180	+1	1.071
August	227	+3	1.041	180	-0-	1.071
September	227	-0-	1.041	182	+2	1.083
October	230	+3	1.055	184	+2	1.095
November	233	+3	1.069	185	+1	1.101
December	235	+2	1.078	186	+1	1.107
1990 Average	224	N/A	N/A	179	N/A	N/A

*Million dollars
**Largest monthly deposit loss
***Largest monthly increase in loans

weekly, and monthly deposit losses during the past several years. Applying the same procedure to the loan portfolio, management can identify the largest daily, weekly, and monthly surge in funding requirements as new lending activity and advances on lines of credit exceeded the principal payments on existing loans. Combining the results of these analyses provides management with an estimate based on recent history of the amount of liquidity required to be available to meet the unexpected demand for cash generated by the normal daily operations of the institution.

Seasonal liquidity requirements can be derived from the same data that was used to determine the short-term liquidity needs. In Table 8.3, columns three and six list the monthly change in deposits and loans of a sample bank during the years 1988 through 1990. Dividing the monthly balance by the prior year's average total deposits or loans produces a monthly index (columns four and seven) for each year. The seasonal trends can easily be discerned by graphing each year's monthly indices on a common graph for deposits (Figure 8.3) and a common graph for loans (Figure 8.4). The graphs indicate a general decline in deposits during the first four months of the year and an increase in lending activity in the spring and fall. Management must be aware of these seasonal trends in order to provide adequate liquidity. To incorporate the seasonal trends into the financial institution's projected cash flow analysis, seasonal adjustment factors can be obtained by averaging each month's index (Table 8.4). If in the 1991 business plan management expects deposits to increase from $235 million at year-end 1990 to $250 million on December 31, 1991, the deposit growth pattern can be forecast by using the seasonal deposit adjustment factors (Table 8.5). When working with projected data, the index

194

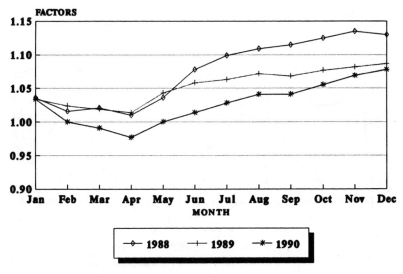

Figure 8.3 Seasonal adjustment factors—deposits

base used in the analysis is not the prior year's average, but rather the projected balance at the end of the year divided by the index for that month. In the example in Table 8.5, the index value at 1.000 is determined by dividing the projected deposit balance on December 31, 1991 by the December index of 1.098 ($250 ÷ 1.098 = $227.7). The seasonally adjusted monthly balances (last column of Table 8.5) can then be determined by multiplying each monthly seasonal factor by the basic index value of 227.7. The projected monthly deposit balances integrate management's deposit growth expectations for 1991 with seasonal growth patterns. When the same analysis is applied to loans, the 1991 business plan can be used to produce a cash flow analysis that will enable the liquidity managers to anticipate the magnitude of the seasonal variations in the institution's liquidity needs.

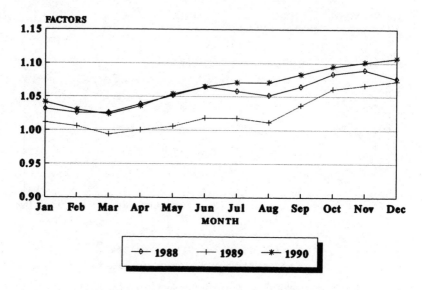

Figure 8.4 Seasonal adjustment factors—loans

The seasonally adjusted deposit and loan projections can be combined with other primary sources and uses of cash, such as fixed income maturities and anticipated asset sales to produce a general cash flow projection for the financial institution (see Table 8.6). If the A/L managers have access to an A/L modeling system capable of producing a projected cash flow analysis, they can integrate the seasonal adjustment factors into the model. This will enable the model to produce cash flow projections that will anticipate the seasonal liquidity requirements.

The projected cash flow analysis should be carefully reviewed at least once each quarter by the ALCO. If the actual changes in total loans and deposits do not correlate well with the projected changes, the ALCO must determine

Table 8.4 Seasonal Adjustment Factors

Month	Deposits				Loans			
	1988	1989	1990	Average	1988	1989	1990	Average
January	1.036	1.034	1.034	1.035	1.032	1.012	1.042	1.029
February	1.016	1.024	1.000	1.013	1.026	1.006	1.030	1.021
March	1.021	1.029	.991	1.010	1.026	.994	1.024	1.015
April	1.010	1.014	.977	1.000	1.039	1.000	1.036	1.025
May	1.036	1.043	1.000	1.026	1.052	1.006	1.054	1.037
June	1.078	1.058	1.014	1.050	1.065	1.018	1.065	1.050
July	1.099	1.063	1.028	1.063	1.058	1.018	1.071	1.049
August	1.109	1.072	1.041	1.074	1.052	1.012	1.071	1.045
September	1.115	1.068	1.041	1.075	1.065	1.037	1.083	1.062
October	1.125	1.077	1.055	1.086	1.084	1.061	1.095	1.080
November	1.135	1.082	1.069	1.095	1.090	1.067	1.101	1.086
December	1.130	1.087	1.078	1.098	1.077	1.073	1.107	1.086

Table 8.5 Projected Deposit Growth for 1991
Seasonally Adjusted

Month	Seasonal Factor × Value @ 1.000 = Projected Monthly Balance			
January	1.035	×	227.7	= 236
February	1.013	×	227.7	= 231
March	1.010	×	227.7	= 230
April	1.000	×	227.7	= 228
May	1.026	×	227.7	= 234
June	1.050	×	227.7	= 239
July	1.063	×	227.7	= 242
August	1.074	×	227.7	= 245
September	1.075	×	227.7	= 245
October	1.086	×	227.7	= 247
November	1.095	×	227.7	= 249
December	1.098	×	227.7	= 250

if it is a brief onetime occurrence, a shift in seasonal trends, or a structural change occurring in the institution's balance sheet. By including the senior executives responsible for the lending and deposit functions as members of the ALCO, the committee can have a more meaningful discussion as to why the actual liquidity needs may not be the same as the projections.

A structural liquidity requirement differs from seasonal and short term liquidity requirements, in that it is not self-correcting over time. Structural liquidity requirements occur as a result of a permanent shift in a financial institution's balance sheet composition. New competitors entering an institution's service area, new financial products offered by non-banking entities, and major changes in the condition of regional economies caused, perhaps, by a major employer leaving the area, can all lead to structural changes in a financial institution's balance sheet that could create a demand for liquidity. Because structural liquidity requirements are caused by permanent changes in an institution's financial structure, short-term borrowing arrangements, such as those used to meet daily and seasonal liquidity requirements, are not appropriate. Available cash, maturing fixed-income investments, and the sale of assets are the primary sources of structural liquidity.

After the magnitude and nature of an institution's liquidity requirements have been determined, the A/L managers must take an inventory of the institution's available liquidity. The most obvious sources of liquidity are excess cash loaned overnight as federal funds sold and maturing securities. Less obvious liquidity sources are federal agency guaranteed loans, which can be sold with relative ease, and fixed-income securities with short-term maturities that can be sold with no more than a small loss during periods of high interest rates.

Each A/L management team must determine what constitutes a small loss when deciding which assets to identify as possible sources of liquidity. To aid in this process, Figure 8.5 illustrates the price erosion occuring in fixed-income instruments bearing an 8% coupon with maturities ranging from one to thirty years when interest rates increase 200 basis points.

In the traditional view of liquidity, a fixed-income instrument identified as a source of liquidity must be readily marketable, unpledged, and have a relatively short maturity. This traditional definition of liquidity is appropriate to use when determining sources of structural liquidity because the fixed-income instruments must be liquidated to provide

Table 8.6 Projected Cash Flow Analysis vs. Actual (in millions)

Month	Total Deposits		Total Loans*		Net Source (+) or Use (−) from Deposits and Loans		Fixed Inc Maturities	Proj Asset Sale	Cash Required − or Provided +	
	Proj.	Act.	Proj.	Act.	Proj.	Act.			Proj.	Act.
January 1990	−3	−4	0	1	−3	−3	5	—	2	2
February	−5	−3	1	2	−4	−1	0	—	−4	−1
March	−1	−2	1	1	0	−1	0	—	0	−1
April	−2	−3	−2	−2	−4	−5	0	—	−4	−5
May	6	5	−2	−3	4	2	0	—	4	2
June	5	3	−2	−2	3	1	0	—	3	1
July	3	3	0	−1	3	2	0	—	3	2
August	2	3	1	0	3	3	0	—	3	3
September	0	0	−3	−2	−3	−2	5	—	2	3
October	2	3	−3	−2	−1	1	0	—	−1	1

November	2	3	-1	-1	1	2	0	—	1	2
December	1	2	0	-1	1	1	0	—	1	1
January 1991	1		-4		-3		5	0	2	
February	-5		2		-3		0	2	-1	
March	-1		1		0		0	0	0	
April	-2		-2		-4		0	0	-4	
May	6		-2		4		0	0	4	
June	5		-2		3		0	0	3	
July	3		0		3		0	0	3	
August	3		1		4		0	0	4	
September	0		-4		-4		5	0	1	
October	2		-3		-1		0	0	-1	
November	2		-1		1		0	0	1	
December	1		0		1		10	0	11	
Total Cash Supplied (required) in 1991	15		-14		1		20	2	23	

*A monthly decline in total loans outstanding is reported here as a positive number because a decline in the loan portfolio is a source of cash and this is a cash flow statement.

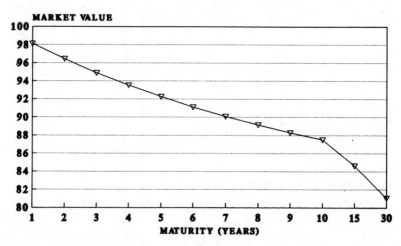

MARKET VALUE

Figure 8.5 Decline in market value of 8% fixed income security when interest rates increase 200 basis points

funds for a long-term change in the balance sheet structure. However, the traditional definition of liquidity is inappropriate to assess the sources of short-term and seasonal liquidity. A long-term fixed-rate government security cannot be counted as a source of structural liquidity, yet it can be identified as a source of short-term and seasonal liquidity because it can be used as collateral to secure short-term borrowings such as reverse repurchase agreements.

It is essential to differentiate between structural liquidity sources and seasonal and short-term liquidity sources when compiling an inventory of an institution's liquidity. Some liquidity sources, such as federal funds sold and securities maturing within 90 days, can be used to satisfy both structural and seasonal liquidity and short-term needs. However, Treasury and agency securities with maturities greater than two years are only counted as short-term and seasonal liquidity sources. Corporate fixed-income securities with maturities between 90 days and two years are a source of liquidity for structural requirements but are not regarded as a liquidity source for short-term and seasonal requirements. Although they can be sold with at worst a small loss, they cannot be used as collateral for reverse repurchase agreements. Various sources of structural liquidity and short-term and seasonal liquidity are listed in Table 8.7. The list of sources of structural liquidity begins with sources that produce no loss and concludes with those sources that could produce the

Table 8.7 Available Liquidity—12/31/90 ($ Millions)

	Sources of Structural Liquidity
4.0	Federal Funds Sold
5.0	Securities Maturing within 180 days that are not pledged
10.0	Securities Maturing in 180 days–1 year that are not pledged
12.0	Student Loans Available for sale
25.0	FNMA/FHLMC PC ARMS that are not pledged
20.0	Securities maturing in 1 year–2 years that are not pledged
76.0	Total

	Sources of Short-Term and Seasonal Liquidity
4.0	Federal Funds Sold
5.0	Non-Treasury or agency securities maturing within 90 days that are not pledged
60.0	Treasuries and Agency securities that are not pledged
30.0	Federal Funds Borrowing Lines
99.0	Total

largest acceptable loss and still be counted as a source of structural liquidity.

The liquidity analysis culminates when the institution's projected cash flow is combined with its current federal funds balance (Table 8.8). The projected sources and uses of funds for the next 12 months is determined by adding together the projected monthly cash flows for January through December as listed in Table 8.6. Utilizing any of the other potential sources of liquidity will not happen automatically. If additional liquidity is needed, action will be required by the institution's management team. To provide additional liquidity, management must determine the nature of any liquidity demand and design an action plan using either the structural or seasonal liquidity sources listed in Table 8.7. The example used in Table 8.8 will not require management to provide additional liquidity because the anticipated cash flow of the institution during the next 12 months will supply $23 million of liquidity in addition to the $4 million of federal funds sold.

Another way liquidity can be measured is by the speed with which it can be supplied. Federal funds are available to meet liquidity needs each day, if Treasury securities are sold they will settle on the next business day, corporate securities

Table 8.8 Projected Liquidity Requirement ($ Millions)

23.0	Projected source or (use) of cash during the next twelve months
+ 4.0	Federal funds sold (+) or purchased(−)
27.0	Liquidity available or (required) during the next 12 months

settle in one week, the sale of whole loans may take up to one month to negotiate and settle; and the sale lease-back of a building can take up to three months or more to complete. Table 8.9 provides a sample report in which a bank has examined its sources of liquidity to determine how quickly liquidity can be provided. Just because an asset is marketable and can be sold for little or no loss does not mean it is a source of funds to meet short-term liquidity needs. Financial institutions using the traditional approach to liquidity mea-

Table 8.9 Liquidity Source Timing Report ($ Millions)

Source	Number of Days Until Liquidity is Available				
	Same	1	2–7	8–30	Over 30
Federal Funds Sold	4.0				
Sell Short-Term Treasury Securities		5.0			
Sell Short-Term Corporate Securities			10.0		
Sell Student Loans			12.0		
Sell FNMA/FHLMC ARMS			25.0		
Repo Treasury and Agency Securities	60.0				
Borrow Federal Funds	30.0				
Sell Whole Loan ARMS				25.0	
Sale and Lease-Back of Buildings					15.0
Issue Securities (Stock/Notes)					20.0
Total Liquidity Available by Period	94.0	5.0	47.0	25.0	35.0

surement (listing assets that can be sold for little or no loss) should incorporate the liquidity source timing report into their short term liquidity measurement process. The traditional approach may give the impression that there is ample liquidity to meet immediate short-term requirements when, in fact, that may not be the case.

To condense a financial institution's liquidity position to a single number that can then be used to compare its liquidity with those of other financial institutions, bank analysts use various balance sheet ratios. These ratios are very broad in scope and frequently fail to distinguish between sources of structural liquidity and sources of short-term and seasonal liquidity. Nevertheless, A/L managers must monitor them because they do facilitate the comparison of various financial institutions' liquidity positions and can affect a financial institution's stock price when they are used by bank stock analysts to assess an institution's liquidity risk position.

The following are the most commonly used balance sheet ratios employed by bank stock analysts as a measure of liquidity:

$$\frac{\text{Net Loans}}{\text{Total Deposits}} = X\%$$

$$\frac{\text{Non-Deposit Liabilities}}{\text{Total Liabilities}} = X\%$$

$$\frac{\text{Liquid Assets}}{\text{Total Assets}} = X\%$$

$$\text{Liquid Assets} = \text{cash and due from banks} + \text{deposits placed with banks}$$

+ Treasury securities
+ Federal agency securities
+ trading account securities
+ Federal funds sold
+ commercial paper securities
+ repurchase agreements

$$\frac{\text{Liquid Assets}}{\text{Deposits + short-term borrowings}} = X\%$$

Short-term borrowings = federal funds purchased
     + reverse repurchase agreements
     + other short-term borrowings

There is no one correct way to measure liquidity. It is a matter of judgment. Some A/L managers count intermediate-term Treasury notes as a source of liquidity if the market value is equal to or greater than the book value, others do not. Some A/L managers consider un-mortgaged banking facilities as a source of liquidity. It is the responsibility of each bank's senior management team to use its best judgment to determine what constitutes liquidity. It is also important to understand how the bank regulatory bodies governing a financial institution define liquidity. A/L managers must either have the regulators accept their definition of what constitutes liquidity or conform with the one used by the regulators.

Once the management team determines what constitutes liquidity they must decide how much liquidity must be maintained to provide for the institution's liquidity needs. If an institution is too conservative and maintains a very large liquidity position, its earnings will usually suffer. Generally speaking, liquid assets such as Treasury notes produce a lower return than illiquid assets such as consumer loans. This is why an excessive liquidity position has a real cost associated with it in the form of lower earnings. However, if an institution is too agressive in pursuing income by maintaining a very small liquidity position, it is jeopardizing the very existence of the financial institution.

There are two basic approaches to forecasting a financial institution's liquidity requirements, both of which must be utilized in order to successfully manage the institution's liquidity. The primary forecast is the one most likely to occur. This projection is derived from the institution's history of liquidity requirements combined with the institution's annual business plan for the coming year. If the plan is developed in a thoughtful and realistic manner, the resulting cash flow will provide management with the most realistic estimate of liquidity requirements during the next fiscal year. This is the approach that has been described earlier in this section and is illustrated in Tables 8.3 through 8.8.

The second approach to forecasting liquidity requirements is to employ the worst-case scenario. The scenario is usually based on the greatest liquidity drain the institution has experienced during the past five or ten years or may be based on another financial institution's experience. In the worst-case scenario, it is assumed all credit to the institution will be withdrawn. Therefore, all federal funds lines, maturing reverse repurchase agreements, or any other short-term borrowings will not be counted as a source of seasonal and short-term liquidity. The scenario also assumes a certain percent of the transaction accounts and maturing CDs will be withdrawn from the institution. To develop a worst-case scenario, management must anticipate events that have a very small probability of actually occurring. Therefore, the worst-case scenario is more a judgment call than the result of a scientific process.

The evaluation of most senior management teams is based on their ability to generate income. To accomplish this, they tend to reduce the institution's liquidity position. In contrast, bank regulators are responsible for protecting the customer's deposits by making sure the institution remains solvent. Therefore, they want a relatively large liquidity position to be maintained. Ideally, the contrasting priorities of management and regulators will create a compromise position that will enhance income while providing enough liquidity for the institution to safely operate. A successful liquidity policy will balance the desire to increase interest income with the need to provide adequate liquidity.

ASSET QUALITY ANALYSIS

Much of the value of the banking process is created by managing credit risk. Funds obtained from depositors are used to advance loans to borrowers at substantially higher rates than are being paid on the deposits. Drawing on their expertise and experience in lending, the loan officers and credit review committies approve loans they believe will be repaid as agreed. However, there are several factors that can cause loans to become delinquent, among them are poor underwriting procedures and credit judgment.

The most common cause of borrowers becoming unable to repay their loans is change in the economic environment. This can be as specific as an individual losing his or her job or as general as an industry or even an entire regional or national economy encountering financial difficulty due to factors such as increased foreign competition or a recession in the economy. During periods of expansion the robust business climate will mask all but the most extreme credit mismanagement. However, when the economy turns into recession, banks will experience an increase in loan delinquencies and those with a weak credit management process will encounter the most problems.

Banking, by its very nature, is a highly leveraged situation. Banks are using depositors' funds and other borrowed money to fund loans and investments and are supporting the entire arbitrage with a relatively small amount of capital. At many banks, capital amounts to no more than 7% of their total assets. The highly leveraged position of financial institutions makes them very vulnerable to credit risk. If a bank had 10% of its loans default, the bank's capital could be completely decimated. Even though 90% of the loans were being serviced as agreed, the 10% that were charged off could destroy the bank. An institution's risk exposure is not confined to the loss that may occur when the collateral (if any) is sold for less than the balance of the loan. Before the loan is liquidated it becomes a nonearning asset, which reduces the overall return on assets and causes the net interest margin to compress. Also, delinquent loans require a great deal of lawyers' and management's time, which causes the instutiton's operating expenses to increase. When loan delinquencies increase, a triple squeeze on an institution's net income occurs.

There are some steps that the senior management team can take to reduce the risk that deteriorating credits will severely impact the bank. The first step is to review the bank officers authorized to approve credit. If management is not satisfied that each officer will exercise reasonable judgment when approving loans, the loan officers should be replaced by experienced, conservative lenders whose judgment in approving loans is trusted. After management is satisfied with the caliber of the individuals authorized to approve loans, policies and procedures that will ensure the credit risk managers' expertise is applied to the credit approval process must be put in place. The credit review and approval procedures should be clearly described in a policy and procedures statement and must be checked for compliance during audits.

Even though a bank has experienced and conservative lenders operating within a well-designed credit approval process, serious problems can arise when the economic environment turns negative if the loans are concentrated in an adversely affected industry or geographic area. One way to reduce this risk is to establish a policy that restricts the percent of the loan portfolio that can be in any one area or industry. Although this works in theory, it is frequently not a realistic approach to the problem. Many times an institution's service area will be dominated by a single industry, such as agriculture or automobile manufacturing, or be directed to a specific sector by its founding charter, as is the case with the savings and loan industry, which is committed to lend to the real estate sector.

For a long time, there was not much that could be done to avoid loan concentrations except to restrict lending, which would cause a decline in the net interest income. As a result, savings and loan associations would experience problems when the local real estate market became weak, Michigan banks would encounter difficulty when the auto industry turned down, and Midwestern banks would be faced with serious loan losses when the agricultural sector faltered. Eventually, the fixed-income market evolved to the point where government agencies like the Federal National Mortgage Association (FNMA), Federal Home Loan Mortgage Corporation (FHLMC), Student Loan Marketing Association (SLMA) and the Small Business Association (SBA) were created. These agencies enabled financial institutions to transform unmarketable whole loans into marketable securities guaranteed by the United States government or one of its agencies. The government guarantees permitted banks to remove the credit risk from their balance sheets at a very small cost by converting whole loans into government or agency guaranteed securities. More recently, the creation of asset backed securities using credit card loans or automobile loans to create pass-through securities have further enhanced the ability of financial institutions to manage their credit risk. Regional banks can achieve geographic diversification by creating asset-backed securities with their credit card and automobile loan portfolios, sell a portion of the loans as asset-backed securities, then use the proceeds to purchase similar asset-backed securities issued by banks in other areas of the country. Institutions can also reduce a concentration of one loan type by securitizing it, selling it, and using the proceeds to purchase other types of loans. Credit risk can be reduced by converting existing mortgages into pass-through certificates and holding them in the investment portfolio as agency guaranteed pass-through certificates. In effect, this transfers the credit risk to FHLMC and FNMA in exchange for a small annual guarantee fee. An additional benefit of converting loans into securities arises from the fact that the securities are readily marketable. By securitizing its loan portfolio an institution also improves its liquidity position and makes additional assets available for pledging or collateral for short-term loans. For very large commercial loans, banks can reduce the risk of lending a large amount of money to one borrower by permitting other banks to participate in making the loan.

It is difficult to estimate the amount of credit risk in a bank's balance sheet. Whether an analyst is an outside consultant or a member of the bank's management team, it is impossible to foresee which loans will encounter difficulty in the future. By using current data in conjunction with historical data, analysts can discern trends of deteriorating or improving credit conditions in an institution's balance sheet, discover relative credit risk by comparing the data with the data of similar financial institutions and determine an institution's ability to absorb future loan losses by examining the reserve for loan losses and the capital position. To assist them in this process, analysts have developed various ratios, some of which are described in Table 8.10.

Although it is not in the realm of the asset/liability management committee to manage credit risk, no self-analysis would be complete without examining the institution's credit risk. Credit risk is perhaps the single greatest risk encountered by financial institutions. To be effective in managing the balance sheet the ALCO must be aware of the institution's credit risk exposure. For example, if an institution has a large concentration of floating rate construction loans in its loan portfolio, it would not be a good strategy for the A/L managers to suggest expanding the construction loan portfolio even though it might be the most profitable way to grow the assets and increase the institution's asset sensitivity.

Table 8.10 Ratios Used to Determine Asset Quality

The Amount of Concentration in the Loan and Investment Portfolios:	Recent Credit Experience:	An Institution's Ability to Absorb Loan Losses
$\dfrac{\text{Construction Loans}}{\text{Total Loans}}$	$\dfrac{\text{Net Charge-offs}}{\text{Average Loans}}$	$\dfrac{\text{Nonperforming Assets Less Reserve for Loan Losses}}{\text{Tangible Capital}}$
$\dfrac{\text{Commercial Loans}}{\text{Total Loans}}$	$\dfrac{\text{Nonperforming Assets}}{\text{Total Assets}}$	$\dfrac{\text{Provision for Loan Losses}}{\text{Net Charge-offs}}$
$\dfrac{\text{Foreign Loans}}{\text{Total Loans}}$	$\dfrac{\text{Recoveries in Year X}}{\text{Gross Charge-offs in Year X-1}}$	$\dfrac{\text{Net Charge-offs}}{\text{Average Total Loans}}$
$\dfrac{\text{Real Estate Loans, etc.}}{\text{Total Loans}}$		
$\dfrac{\text{Largest Loan to One Borrower}}{\text{Total Capital}}$		
$\dfrac{\text{Corporate Bonds}}{\text{Total Investments}}$		
$\dfrac{\text{Equity Investments}}{\text{Total Investments}}$		
$\dfrac{\text{Foreign Securities, etc.}}{\text{Total Investments}}$		
$\dfrac{\text{Largest Investment in One Corp.}}{\text{Total Capital}}$		

CAPITAL ANALYSIS

The role of capital in a bank's financial structure is to act as a cushion to absorb the shock of losses. The more capital a bank has, the better it is able to absorb losses. For thinly capitalized banks, relatively minor losses can seriously deplete its capital position. Therefore, banks must maintain a certain amount of capital in order to operate. If a bank had no capital, any net loss would impair its ability to honor its depositors' claims. This observation raises two critical questions: 1.) what comprises a bank's capital? and 2.) how much capital is required to adequately protect the depositors against possible losses?

Bank regulators determine what elements of a bank's balance sheet constitute capital. They approach the process by dividing capital into its two basic components. Tier 1 capital is the core capital position and includes common equity, perpetual preferred stock, and minority interest less goodwill. Tier 2 capital is primarily capital that has been obtained by borrowings. It includes subordinate debt, term preferred stock, and various other capital instruments. Table 8.11 details the components of Tier 1 and Tier 2 capital.

In the past, the minimum amount of capital deemed by regulators as adequate to operate a financial institution was 6% of total assets. This approach failed to consider risk variations between financial institutions that can dramatically change the amount of capital required to cushion the institution against losses resulting from the risks inherent in its balance sheet. Such risks include credit risk, interest rate risk, and liquidity risk. A bank with conservative credit policies, a low exposure to interest rate risk, a large liquidity

Table 8.11 Capital Components

Components	Minimum Requirements
Core primary, Tier 1 capital[1]	Must be equal to or exceed 4% of weighted risk assets
Common stockholders' equity	No limit
Qualifying cumulative and noncumulative[1] perpetual preferred stock	Limited to 25% of the sum of common stock, minority interests, and qualifying perpetual preferred stock
Minority interest in equity accounts of consolidated subsidiaries	Organizations should avoid using minority interests to introduce elements not otherwise qualifying for Tier 1 capital
Less goodwill	
Supplementary Tier 2 capital:	Total of Tier 2 is limited to 100% of Tier 1[2]
Allowance for loan and lease losses	Limited to 25% of weighted risk assets[2]
Perpetual preferred stock	No limit within Tier 2
Hybrid capital instruments, perpetual debt (for BHCs), equity contract notes (for state member banks), and mandatory convertible securities	No limit within Tier 2
Subordinated debt and intermediate-term stock (original weighted average maturity of 5 years or more	Subordinated debt and intermediate-term preferred stock are limited to 50% of Tier 1,[3] amortized for capital purposes as they approach maturity
Revaluation reserves (equity and building)	Not included; organizations encouraged to disclose may be evaluated on a case-by-case basis for international comparisons and taken into account in making an overall assessment of capital

Deductions (from sum of Tier 1 and Tier 2)

Investments in unconsolidated subsidiaries

As a general rule, one-half of the aggregate investments will be deducted from Tier 1 capital for bank holding companies.[4] For state member banks, deduction is from total capital only

Reciprocal holdings of banking organizations' capital securities

Other deductions (such as other subsidiaries or joint ventures) as determined by supervisory authority

On a case-by-case basis or as a matter of policy after formal rule making

1. For bank holding companies, cumulative perpetual preferred stock will count as Tier 1 capital, subject to certain limits. For state members banks, only noncumulative perpetual preferred stock will count as Tier 1 capital. Cumulative preferred in which accumulated dividends are payable only in the form of common stock will be deemed to be noncumulative preferred for risk-based capital purposes. Dutch-auction preferred stock will not count for Tier 1.

2. Amounts in excess of the limitations are permitted but do not qualify as capital.

3. In the supplementary items such as term subordinated debt and long/intermediate maturity or term preferred stock, the outstanding amount of the capital instrument eligible for inclusion as supplementary capital will be discounted by a fifth of the original amount (less any redemptions) each year during the last 5 years before maturity. Such instruments will have a capital value of zero when they have a remaining maturity of less than a year.

4. A proportionately greater amount may be deducted from Tier 1 capital if the risks associated with the subsidiary so warrant.

position and little, if any, off balance sheet contingencies, will require much less capital to protect its depositors than a bank that incurs a high degree of credit risk in the lending and investment functions, has a high exposure to interest rate risk, maintains a minimum liquidity position, or has a large amount of off balance sheet contingencies.

Regulators have recently abandoned their "one-size-fits-all" policy of requiring financial institutions to maintain a capital to asset ratio of 6% in favor of capital requirements that reflect the varying degree of credit risk in a banks' balance sheet. Each general asset category is assigned a capital requirement that is directly proportional to its per-ceived credit risk (Table 8.12). The new capital regulation now requires banks to maintain a risk-adjusted capital base of at least 8% (Table 8.13). Although this is an improvement over the previous capital requirement regulations, it fails to take into account variations in the amount of interest rate risk that exists between financial institutions.

The ALCO must regularly review the credit risk–adjusted capital ratio to be certain the 8% minimum is maintained. The ALCO must also examine the institution's interest rate risk exposure. If a 200 basis point change up or down in interest rates produces a substantial change in the net interest income, it may be prudent to establish a minimum capital level in excess of the regulatory minimum.

Banking, by its very nature, is a highly leveraged industry. A highly leveraged position is required for the relatively narrow net interest income to cover the operating expenses of the institution and produce a satisfactory return for the shareholders. Financial institutions tend to move toward a more highly leveraged position as they attempt to produce a higher return on their shareholders' equity. Although the

Table 8.12 Capital Risk Weightings

0% Risk Assets	■ Cash (domestic and foreign) held or in transit
	■ Balances due from Federal Reserve Banks (including Federal Reserve Bank stock) and central banks in other OECD countries
	■ Direct claims on, and the portions of claims that are unconditionally guaranteed by; the U.S. Treasury, U.S. government agencies, and the central governments of OECD countries and local currency claims on, and the portions of local currency claims unconditionally guaranteed by the central governments of non-OECD countries (including their central banks), to the extent of the liabilities booked in that currency
	■ Gold bullion in the vaults of the (subsidiary) depository institution or in another's vaults on an allocated basis, to the extent offset by gold bullion liabilities
20% Risk Assets	■ Cash in process of collection
	■ All claims (long- or short-term) on, and the portions of claims (long- or short-term) that are guaranteed by, U.S. depository institutions and OECD banks
	■ Short-term claims (remaining maturity 1 year or less) on, and the portions of short-term claims that are guaranteed by, non-OECD banks
	■ Portions of claims that are conditionally guaranteed by the central governments of OECD countries and U.S. government agencies, and the portions of claims that are guaranteed by the central governments of non-OECD countries to the extent of liabilities booked in that currency
	■ Claims on, and the portions of claims that are guaranteed by, U.S. government–sponsored agencies

Table 8.12 Capital Risk Weightings (*continued*)

- General obligation claims on, and the portions of claims guaranteed with full faith and credit by, local governments and political subdivisions of the U.S. and other OECD local governments
- Claims on, and the portions of claims that are guaranteed by, official multilateral lending institutions or regional development banks
- The portions of the claims that are collateralized by securities issued or guaranteed by the U.S. Treasury, the central governments of other OECD countries, U.S. government agencies, U.S. government–sponsored agencies, or by cash on deposit in the (subsidiary) institution
- The portions of the claims that are collateralized by securities issued by official mulutilateral lending institutions or regional development banks
- Certain privately issued securities representing indirect ownership of mortgage-backed U.S. government agency or U.S. government–sponsored agency securities
- Investments in shares of a fund whose portfolio is permitted to hold only securities that would qualify for the 0% or 20% risk categories

50% Risk Assets
- Loans fully secured by first liens on 1–4 family residential properties that have been made in accordance with prudent underwriting standards, that are performing in accordance with their original terms, and are not past due or in nonaccrual status, and the certain privately issued, mortgage-backed securities represeting indirect ownership of such loans (excluding loans made for speculative purposes)

220

Table 8.12 Capital Risk Weightings (*continued*)

	■ Revenue bonds or similar claims that are obligations of U.S. state or local governments or other OECD local governments, but for which the government entity is committed to repay the debt only out of the revenues from the facilities financed
	■ Credit-equivalent amounts of interest rate and foreign-exchange rate related contracts that do not qualify for inclusion in a lower risk category
100% Risk Assets	■ All other claims on private obligors
	■ Claims on, or guaranteed by, non-OECD banks with a remaining maturity exceeding 1 year
	■ Claims on, or guaranteed by, non-OECD central governments that are not included in item (3) of the 0% category or item (4) of the 20% category; all claims on non-OECD state or local governments
	■ Obligations issued by U.S. state or local governments, or other OECD local governments (including industrial development authorities and similar entities) repayable solely by a private party or enterprise
	■ Premises, plant, and equipment; other fixed assets; and other real estate owned
	■ Investments in any unconsolidated subsidiaries, joint ventures, or associated companies, if not deducted from capital
	■ Instruments issued by other banking organizations, if not deducted from capital
	■ Claims on commercial firms owned by a government
	■ All other assets, including any intangible assets that are not deducted from capital

Table 8.13 Minimum Capital Requirements

Category	Requirement
A. Minimum standard of total capital to weighted risk assets	8.0%
B. Minimum standard of Tier 1 capital to weighted risk assets	4.0%
C. Minimum standard of stockholders equity to weighted risk assets	4.0%
D. Limitations on supplementary capital elements	
1. Allowance for loan and lease losses	1.25% of weighted risk assets
2. Perpetual preferred stock	No limit within Tier 2
3. Hybrid capital perpetual debt (for BHCs) equity contract notes (for state member banks), and mandatory convertibles	No limit within Tier 2
4. Subordinated debt and intermediate term preferred stock	Combined maximum of 50% of Tier 1
5. Total qualifying Tier 2 capital	May not exceed Tier 1 capital
E. Definition of total capital	Tier 1 plus Tier 2 less: reciprocal holdings of banking organizations' capital instruments and investments in unconsolidated subsidiaries[1]

1. 50% of the aggregate amount of investments will be deducted from Tier 1 capital if the risks associated with the subsidiary so warrant.

drift toward highly leveraged positions is limited by regulatory minimum capital requirements, management must go beyond the regulatory minimums, which are based solely on credit risk exposure, and assess the total risk exposure of the institution when determining how much capital is adequate to protect the depositors. Each financial institution will have to determine how much capital is required to be prudent because no two financial institutions have the same exposure to risks.

9

Asset/Liability Management
In Action

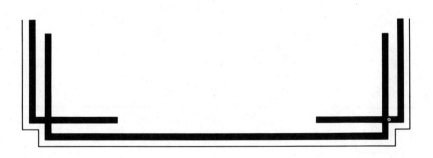

Asset/Liability management activities fall into two general categories, defensive and pro-active. The most common use of asset/liability management is as a defensive process. A/L managers run the computer simulation models using various interest rate scenarios and if the income, liquidity position, the net value of portfolio equity or capital ratios move beyond policy limits, they consider implementing an action plan. The process can also be used in a pro-active manner as a strategic planning tool. A/L managers can use the simulation model to test various asset mixes and funding combinations as well as price/volume relationships. When one of the simulations increases the net interest income without causing a corresponding increase in the institution's overall risk profile, a plan of action is implemented that will convert the simulation into reality. Financial institutions using A/L management in a defensive manner usually remain profitable viable institutions. However, institutions using A/L management as a pro-active strategic planning tool as well as a defensive tool can often be found in the upper quartile on performance measurement reports.

DEFENSIVE ACTIONS

Many financial institutions and most regulatory authorities use a static rate scenario to measure interest rate risk exposure. Current interest rates are moved up and down by a fixed amount and model simulation reports are produced for each rate scenario. This approach works well as long as interest rates are in the middle of their historical range. However, when interest rates move to the lower end of their range, adhering to static rate scenario testing can produce distorted results. If these results are used as the basis for an action plan, inappropriate actions might be taken. For example, if the current level of short-term interest rates is 9%, a rate shock test of plus or minus 400 basis points is not unreasonable. But, if current short-term rates are 5%, applying a rate shock of down 400 basis points would place short-term rates at 1%. There could be extreme situations where short-term rates might reach 1%, but a review of the past movements of interest rates indicates this has an extremely low probability of occurring. To base an action plan on an interest rate scenario that is highly unlikely to occur is a dangerous practice. It is more useful to use interest rate scenarios that are the extreme to which current rates could realistically move. For example, if current short-term interest rates are 5%, a realistic interest rate shock test might be a low of 3% and a high of 9%.

To measure an institution's interest rate risk exposure, the various interest rate scenarios are applied to a projected balance sheet structure. The institution's business plan for the next year is the most reliable basis for projecting the future structure of the balance sheet because it reflects management's best estimate of future loan and deposit activity. If all the rate scenarios produce income greater than the lowest acceptable limit and do not cause the value of portfolio equity to decline below the lowest acceptable limit, no defensive action is warranted. However, if one of the rate scenarios causes any of the lowest acceptable limits to be violated, as defined in the asset/liability management policy, defensive action may be required.

It should be noted that action should not automatically be taken when model simulation results violate a financial limit. The violation should, however, prompt intense analysis of the situation and be thoroughly discussed with the ALCO to determine whether the simulation is accurate. If the model simulation results are found to be accurate, the ALCO must decide what actions will be most effective in resolving the problem.

A convenient way to monitor financial limits is to include the limit for each category on the corresponding graph of the dynamic simulation analysis results. Figure 9.1 illustrates the impact on an institution's net interest income when rates rise 400 basis points, decline 400 basis points, or remain unchanged, and charts the lowest acceptable limit. If the ALCO establishes the lowest acceptable monthly net interest income they are willing to tolerate for any realistic rate scenario at $26 million and rates fall 400 basis points, the graph indicates that the monthly net interest income limit would be violated within a few months. This situation should be the main focus

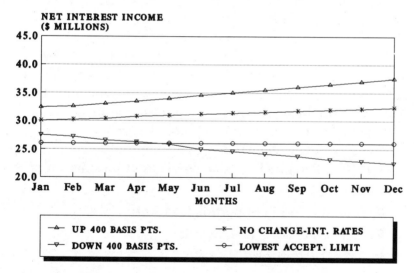

Figure 9.1 Dynamic simulation analysis results

of the next ALCO meeting, or if the asset/liability manager deems the situation to be critical, a special session of the ALCO should be convened to discuss the problem.

At the ALCO meeting, the first order of business is to determine whether the interest rate scenario that caused the limit violation has a reasonable probability of actually occurring. Members of the ALCO should also carefully examine the assumptions driving the model such as basis risk parameters, variations in embedded options, and projected balance sheet structure changes to be certain they are still applicable. If the ALCO determines the interest rate scenario has a reasonable chance of occurring and the model assumptions are valid, the committee may elect to take corrective action.

If the ALCO is convinced action is required to alter the outcome predicted by the simulation model, the committee must develop and implement strategies that will bring the simulation model results into compliance with the policy limits. The institution illustrated in Figure 9.1 is an asset-sensitive institution. Therefore, if the amount of its asset sensitivity can be reduced, the deterioration of the net interest income will be less as interest rates decline. Although the amount of increase in net interest income as interest rates rise would also be reduced, preventing the net interest income from falling to unacceptable levels as rates decline 400 basis points is the ALCO's top priority.

Possible strategies for reducing the asset sensitivity are:

- Extend investment portfolio maturities
- Increase floating-rate deposits
- Increase short-term deposits
- Increase fixed-rate lending

- Sell adjustable-rate loans
- Increase short-term debt
- Increase floating rate long-term debt
- Enter into an interest rate swap (receive a fixed rate and pay a floating rate)
- Purchase an interest rate floor contract

Each strategy must be carefully examined by the ALCO to determine its impact on the risk profile and financial structure of the institution. Although any of the strategies mentioned above will reduce the asset-sensitive position of the institution, some, such as increasing deposits, will create a source of new funds that must then be profitably invested while others, such as increasing fixed-rate lending, might strain the institution's liquidity position by requiring funding. Each strategy also has different credit risks that will affect the amount of risk-based capital an institution is required to maintain. The strategy of increasing fixed-rate loans on the balance sheet will expose the institution to more credit risk than the strategy of extending Treasury note maturities in the investment portfolio. All of these issues must be carefully considered when selecting appropriate strategies to reduce the institution's asset sensitivity.

The ALCO must determine which strategies are possible to use. For example, if there is no customer demand for floating-rate deposits or fixed-rate loans, it will not be possible for the institution to use them to reduce its asset sensitivity position. However, if there are significant amounts of near-term maturities in the investment portfolio, these instruments can be sold and the proceeds used to purchase intermediate-term fixed-rate securities.

Developing an effective marketing program and paying premium short-term deposit rates would help the institution reduce its asset-sensitive position by increasing short-term deposits. It would be ideal if the new short-term deposits could be used to fund intermediate-term fixed-rate loans, but if there is no demand for fixed-rate loans, the funds will be used to purchase intermediate-term securities at lower interest rates than the loans would have earned, which could reduce the net interest margin.

Extending maturities in the investment portfolio does not expand the balance sheet or create a source or use of funds, whereas attracting new short-term deposits expands the balance sheet and creates a source of funds that must be deployed in a manner consistent with the institution's liquidity needs, profit objectives, interest rate risk parameters and credit standards.

The institution can also decide to enter into an interest rate swap agreement under which it will pay a fixed rate of interest and receive a variable interest rate payment, or it can purchase an interest rate floor. Either of these instruments will reduce the institution's asset sensitivity position without inflating the balance sheet or creating a source or use of funds.

An equal dollar amount of each strategy should be tested in the simulation model to determine which strategy most effectively reduces the institution's interest rate risk exposure. The results of the model simulations will be the basis of discussion to determine the most effective strategies at the next ALCO meeting. Often, the final action plan will consist of more than one strategy. For example, if the asset-sensitive institution depicted in Figure 9.1 wants to reduce its interest rate risk exposure without expanding its balance sheet, it might decide to enter into an interest rate swap agreement and extend the shorter maturities in its investment portfolio.

When the ALCO has agreed to a plan of action, the plan should be tested in the simulation model to be certain the combination of strategies will have the desired effect. If the action plan is effective, the resulting net interest income figures will be similar to those depicted in Figure 9.2. Comparing Figures 9.1 and 9.2 illustrates how the action plan will reduce the volatility of the net interest income, thereby raising the institution's net interest income above the lowest acceptable limit when interest rates decline 400 basis points. The plan will, unfortunately, reduce the amount of increase in the net interest income if interest rates increase 400 basis points, but this is the cost of reducing its interest rate

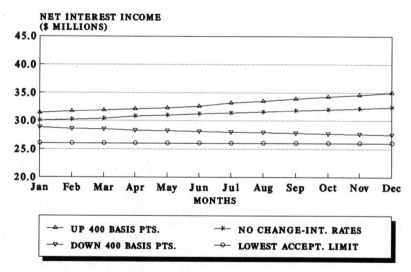

Figure 9.2 Dynamic Simulation Analysis Results

risk. The information contained in Figure 9.2 indicates the action plan is effective and should be implemented.

The ALCO must set a time frame for implementing the action plan and assign to appropriate individuals the responsibility for executing the plan. The A/L manager must closely monitor the plan's implementation and provide a progress report at each ALCO meeting. Upon completion of the action plan, it is the A/L manager's responsibility to furnish the ALCO with a full report comparing the actual implementation of the plan with the plan as originally approved by the committee. Periodically, the A/L manager should update the ALCO on the actual impact the plan is having on the institution and compare it with what the plan was originally expected to accomplish. In that way the ALCO will be able to learn from their past experiences and determine whether their strategies continue to be effective.

PRO-ACTIVE

Pro-active asset/liability managers do not wait for model simulations to violate a policy limit before recommending action. They continually search for the optimal asset mix, funding combination, and loan and deposit pricing strategies that will produce the largest improvement in the institution's net interest income and net value of portfolio equity. The A/L manager must work with the ALCO members to clearly define the institution's constraints. Many of the optimal strategies will be beyond the various constraints within which the institution must operate. Therefore, those outside the constraints must be discarded.

Capital requirements have long been a constraint on an institution's ability to grow. Given the regulatory agencies' minimum capital requirements, an institution with a nominal capital-to-asset ratio will be unable to expand its balance sheet. A strategy to expand the deposit base and use the proceeds to fund consumer loans may enhance the institution's net interest income, but must be discarded because it will expand the balance sheet, and in so doing, will violate the regulator's minimum capital ratio requirement.

The minimum risk-adjusted capital ratios established by the regulatory bodies create the possibility that a strategy may violate the capital ratio without expanding the balance sheet. For an institution maintaining a minimum risk-adjusted capital position, a strategy of altering the asset mix by selling Treasury securities and using the proceeds to fund commercial loans is unrealistic. Even though the strategy does not expand the balance sheet, it shifts assets from Treasury securities, which require no capital to support them, into commercial loans that do require additional designated capital. Institutions with relatively low levels of risk-based capital must carefully review strategies involving asset mix changes as well as strategies that cause the balance sheet to expand.

There are two basic ways an institution's liquidity position can limit the use of certain strategies. The strategies can require additional liquidity or reduce the supply of available liquidity. Attracting large amounts of short-term institutional deposits to an institution and using the proceeds to fund floating-rate commercial loans may increase the net interest income without a corresponding increase in interest rate risk; however, it will significantly increase the institution's need to maintain additional liquidity. If the institutional depositors perceive a deterioration in the financial condition of the institution, or if competitors begin to offer much higher rates of interest on their short-term institutional deposits, a significant liquidity drain could occur as the deposits are withdrawn. The same institution could fund its commercial loans with the proceeds of maturing Treasury securities. Although this strategy will not increase the institution's need for liquidity, the loss of the short-term Treasury securities will reduce the available amount of liquid assets. If an institution has a large amount of liquidity in its balance sheet structure, both of these strategies may provide attractive opportunities to reduce the interest rate risk and enhance the institution's net interest income. However, if the institution is currently operating with a low amount of available liquidity, these strategies could create too much liquidity risk and must be discarded.

An institution's ability or willingness to tolerate additional interest rate risk also limits the number of available strategies that can be employed. A strategy causing the net interest income to significantly increase when tested in the simulation model using the most likely and sharply rising interest rate scenarios must be discarded if the interest rate scenario of a sharp decline in interest rates causes it to fall below the minimum acceptable level for the net interest income. Even though significant benefits may be realized by the institution if interest rates increase, the negative impact of a decline in interest rates may be too severe. No one is consistently accurate in predicting interest rates. Therefore, institutions must avoid making big bets on the future direction of interest rates.

In addition to the financial constraints that are usually defined in the institution's asset/liability management policy, there are practical constraints under which the institution must operate. There must be demand for a particular product in order for the institution to increase its sales volume of the product. Using an excess federal funds position to fund a 25% increase in the consumer loan portfolio during the next 12 months could greatly benefit the net interest income and not violate any of the institution's financial constraints; however, if the consumers' demand for loans is weak, the strategy may be unrealistic. The institution can attempt to stimulate demand by reducing the interest rate charged on consumer loans or lower the credit standards so more customers will qualify for loans, but the lower lending rates will erode some of the income advantage offered by consumer loans and the reduced credit standards will increase the institution's exposure to credit risk. New lending activity can usually be stimulated by lowering interest rates and reducing credit standards, however, the additional risks may outweigh the rewards.

The institution's risks must also be reduced by maintaining a diversified balance sheet structure. The fortunes of institutions that depend solely on commercial lending will rise and fall with the business cycle. Institutions involved only in real estate lending may experience serious financial difficulties when the real estate market becomes weak. Institutions totally dependent on consumer lending will suffer when consumer loan demand fades or consumers experience difficulty in repaying their existing loans. The various lending sectors do not always become weak at the same time and even when they do, as happens during a recession, they may not all experience the same magnitude of deterioration. For this reason it is important for institutions to diversify their lending activity. There are no standard ratios that define what constitutes adequate diversification. Every institution's ALCO must decide how the balance sheet is divided between the various loan and deposit products. The A/L manager can then use the committee's decision to identify and reject strategies that are not appropriate because they create too much concentration in one asset type or funding source.

Drawing on their financial skills and experience, proactive asset/liability managers use simulation models to test scenarios that comply with the various financial and practical constraints to determine which scenarios will most favorably impact the institution. The most successful scenarios provide the basis from which the A/L manager can construct an action plan. All scenarios should be tested in the simulation model to determine whether they can improve the institution's financial performance. Some examples are as follows:

- An aggressive marketing program can increase demand deposits by $20 million. At the same time, $20 million of high-cost institutional deposits mature and are not renewed.
- An aggressive marketing program can increase demand deposits by $20 million and the new deposits are used to purchase two-year Treasury notes.
- If the regular savings passbook rate is lowered from 5% to 4%, $25 million of the $115 million in passbook accounts is expected to be withdrawn. Half of the $25 million is expected to leave the bank, and the other half will be deposited in 90-day time deposits.
- The proceeds from $30 million of securities maturing within the next 180 days are used to make adjustable-rate mortgages rather than being reinvested in two-year Treasury notes.

■ Time deposits are priced 50 basis points below the average time deposit rates of the competition. During the next 12 months, $50 million of the $300 million maturing time deposits leave the bank. The runoff will be funded by maturing Treasury securities.

When the simulation model scenario testing has been completed, the most effective scenarios can be combined to form an action plan. Using the financial and practical constraints as a guide, the A/L manager can determine a goal in dollars for each strategy and use the simulation model to test the combined effect of the strategies before proposing them as a formal plan of action. The combination of various strategies occasionally creates a synergy that amplifies the impact of the strategies. For example, the strategy of employing an aggressive marketing promotion to increase the demand deposit base and using the proceeds to fund commercial loans can have a positive synergistic effect on demand deposits. As the institution increases its commercial lending activity, new commercial customers will be attracted to the institution. The new commercial customers will usually transfer their demand deposit accounts to the institution. In this way, the commercial lending program amplifies the increase in the demand deposit accounts. When selecting strategies for inclusion in the action plan, it is important to consider both the positive and negative synergistic relationships that exist between some of the strategies and select strategies with a positive synergistic relationship.

After the A/L manager has identified the most effective strategies for inclusion in the action plan, the plan must be presented to the ALCO for approval. The A/L manager must be certain the ALCO members thoroughly understand the plan. The committee members must not only understand the plan's positive impact on the net interest income, they must also be made aware of the plan's effect on the overall financial risks of the institution. The committee must consider the plan's impact on the institution's liquidity position, exposure to credit risk, interest rate risk, and capital requirements before making a decision to implement the plan.

An effective way to present this information to the ALCO is to produce a full set of financial reports based on the balance sheet as it will appear after the plan is successfully completed. The financial reports should include a balance sheet, projected income statement, liquidity position analysis, capital analysis, and an interest rate risk analysis. The report format should be the same as those used in the standard report package by the ALCO in their regular meetings. The committee members are familiar with these formats and can better understand and compare the information than if it were to be presented using an unfamiliar format.

An effective manner in which to present an action plan's impact on the net interest income is to use a dynamic simulation analysis graph. Using the simulation model to apply the various interest rate scenarios to the balance sheet as it will appear after the action plan is completed reveals the plan's impact on the institution's interest rate risk exposure as reflected by the net interest income. A successful action plan will reduce the volatility of the net interest income produced by the changes in interest rates (Figure 9.2) and/or increase the overall level of the net interest income (Figure 9.3).

If an appropriate action plan is successfully implemented by the financial institution depicted in Figure 9.1, the impact

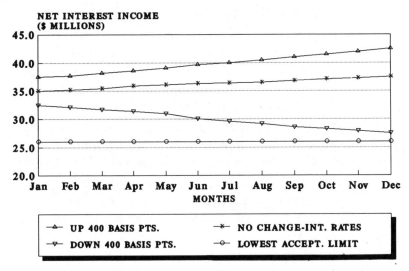

**NET INTEREST INCOME
($ MILLIONS)**

Legend:
- ─▲─ UP 400 BASIS PTS.
- ─▼─ DOWN 400 BASIS PTS.
- ─✳─ NO CHANGE-INT. RATES
- ─○─ LOWEST ACCEPT. LIMIT

Figure 9.3 Dynamic simulation analysis results

on the monthly net interest income would appear as it does in Figure 9.3. In this example, the action plan causes an overall increase in the institution's net interest income. Under the worst-case interest rate scenario, the action plan is sufficient to bring the net interest income above the lowest acceptable limit.

If the ALCO approves the action plan, the committee must establish a time frame for implementing the plan. It is in the best interest of the institution to complete the plan as soon as possible; however, when determining the projected completion date for the plan, the committee members must remember that certain strategies, particularly those requiring a substantial dollar volume or changing customer product preference, will require time to implement.

The ALCO should assign responsibility for implementing the plan to the appropriate individuals. For example, the chief investment officer should be responsible for implementing strategies involving repositioning the investment portfolio, and the chief lending officer should be responsible for executing strategies involving lending. These individuals should provide the ALCO with periodic updates on their progress toward completing the action plan. When the action plan is completed, the individuals responsible for implementing each strategy should make a detailed report to the ALCO. The report compares the actual size, cost, and overall impact of their actions with the strategy as originally approved by the committee.

After an action plan has been implemented, the ALCO should periodically review it to be certain it continues to be effective and appropriate. The structure of an institution's balance sheet and the economic environment in which it operates is in a constant state of flux. A strategy that is currently very beneficial to an institution may work to its detriment two years from now. Strategies must not be implemented and forgotten.

At the present time, there are no simulation models that will accept the various constraints identified by the ALCO and work within those constraints to determine the optimal asset mix, funding combinations, and loan and deposit pricing strategies. However, by using a carefully constructed simulation model, A/L managers, through trial and error, can search for the strategies that will provide the most benefit to the institution. What constitutes an optimal situation is constantly changing. Shifting customer demand for financial products, an ever-changing competitive environment, and the constant movement of interest rates makes the optimal situation an elusive goal. If the most effective asset mix, funding combination, and loan and deposit pricing strategies are achieved today, they will not constitute the most efficient situation one or two years from now. However, those institutions willing to commit the time and energy to move in the direction of an optimal structure will often realize a significant improvement in their net interest income.

USING A CONSULTANT

Many medium and small-sized financial institutions do not have senior managers with asset/liability management experience and do not want to hire a full-time asset/liability manager. For these institutions, an asset/liability management consultant can prove to be extremely beneficial. Some consultants will use the reports generated by the institution's simulation model and help the ALCO evaluate the risk exposure and develop successful strategies to manage the risks. Other consultants only require their clients to furnish them with the institution's financial data. These consultants enter the data into simulation models and provide reports to the ALCO as well as recommend appropriate action strategies.

Extreme care must be exercised when selecting a consultant. There are asset/liability consultants affiliated with firms whose primary business is to sell financial instruments. Many of these consultants operate in the best interest of their clients, however, others may not be able to remain objective and will use the consulting relationship as an entrée to sell the client financial instruments. When selecting a consultant, it is a good practice to check with some of the current clients to find out whether they are satisfied with the consultant's services.

The ALCO must ask the consultants what model they use to conduct their analyses. If the net value of portfolio equity or duration analysis is important to the institution, the ALCO must be certain the consultant's model is capable of providing this information. The ALCO members must determine what reports and graphs they are going to require, then request that the consultant provide sample reports for their review.

The large variety of balance sheet structures and the unique characteristics of every market area make each institution's asset/liability management requirements unique. This is why it is extremely important for the consultant to be an effective listener and not have a one-size-fits-all approach to asset/liability management. The consultant's recommendations and action plans must be tailored to meet the needs of each institution. In addition to being well qualified, the consultant should have good rapport with the members of the ALCO. This will develop trust and make the client's interaction with the consultant more productive.

A CONSTANTLY EVOLVING PROCESS

Asset/liability management is the newest discipline in the field of banking. The concept of lending is thousands of years old. The concept of accepting deposits is hundreds of years old. But the discipline of asset/liability management has existed for only two decades. Because it is in the early stages of its evolution, it is constantly changing. To get the most benefit from the asset/liability management process, the ALCO members must stay current with the latest developments.

Reading periodicals is an excellent way to stay current with new developments in asset/liability management. They are current, easily obtained, and usually clearly and concisely written. They can be found in financial trade publications such as *Bankers Monthly, The American Banker,* and *Bank Management* as well as in the various state associations' publications, or in newsletters like "Bank Asset/Liability Management," published by Warren, Gorham, and Lamont, the "Financial Executives Institute Newsletter," and the "Bank Administration Institute's Monthly Report."

There are also some excellent books available to help the ALCO members become more knowledgeable about asset/liability management. A good introductory text is Thomas Farin's *Asset/Liability Management for Savings Institutions.* For more experienced managers, *Bankers Treasury Management Handbook* by Barrett Binder provides informative reading, as does *Asset/Liability Management,* edited by Frank Fabozzi and Atsuo Konishi.

Asset/liability management seminars are also an effective way to keep informed about current issues. The Bank Administration Institute and the American Bankers Association sponsor excellent asset/liability management seminars each year. The seminars consist of a two- or three-day forum in which experts in the various specialties within the asset/liability management field make presentations and answer questions. An important feature of every seminar is the opportunity to interact with other asset/liability managers. Networking with other attendees is frequently a source of information as valuable as the information received in the formal presentations.

Asset/liability management can be of great benefit to the institutions in which it is employed. However, to realize the full benefit of the process, asset/liability managers and ALCO members must stay current with the new strategies, management techniques, and financial tools that are constantly being created as the asset/liability management process continues to evolve.

BIBLIOGRAPHY

Trade Publications

Bankers Monthly. Published by Hanover Publishers, Inc., New York, NY 10019

The American Banker. Published by Thomson Financial Information, New York, N.Y. 10004

Bank Management. Published by Bank Administration Institute, Chicago, IL 60606.

Bank Accounting & Finance. Published by The John Colet Press Inc., Boston, MA. 02116

Newsletters

"Bank Asset/Liability Management". Published monthly by Warren, Gorham and Lamont, Boston, MA 02111.

"Financial Executives Institute Newsletter." Published by The Financial Executives Research Foundation, Morristown, N.J. 07962

"Bank Administration Institute's Monthly Report". Published by Bank Administration Institute, Chicago, IL 60606.

Books

Farin, Thomas A. *Asset/Liability Management for Savings Institutions.* 1989; The Institute of Financial Education, Chicago, Il 60601.

Binder, Barrett. *Bankers Treasury Management Handbook.* 1988; Warren, Gorham and Lamont, Inc., Boston, MA 02111.

Fabozzi, Frank J. and Konishi, Atsuo (Eds). *Asset/Liability Management.* 1990; Probus Publishing Co., Chicago, IL.

10

Words of Wisdom

Ｎew information and additional insights about the asset/liability management process can frequently be obtained by talking with other A/L managers. In this context, leading authorities in the field of asset/liability management were asked to contribute some thoughts that would be interesting and helpful to those involved in asset/ liability management. Their responses were as follows:

■ Through the decade of the 1990s, banks will continue to face the challenges of economic uncertainty, changing regulation, increasing competition, and industry consolidation. These challenges will provide opportunities for A/L managers who want to move beyond gap analysis and develop additional disciplines to help them survive. Proactive profit management will be one such discipline. Profit management will comprise two key activities—retrospective profitability reporting and prospective pricing simulation. Focused on the individual transaction, these activities will assist banks in the delicate art of pricing loans and deposits in an increasingly competitive market.

Mark Altenbernd, Principal
Profit Management Associates

■ The asset/liability management process should be earnings driven and interpreted. It requires more than engaging in some faddish and disconnected way or exotic intermarket arbitrage or "bear put options." The concept governing the use and objectives of asset/liability management is total rate of return. That is, the balance sheet can be viewed as a mega-investment portfolio diversified into subset portfolios (business, programs, products, and balance sheet items). Management's objective for this portfolio is to maximize net interest income/margin, reinvestment earnings, and capital gains, at all times maintaining as liquid and as marketable a balance sheet as possible.

Barrett F. Binder, President
Global Treasury Associates

■ The goal of asset/liability management is to provide the bank with a stable and competitive return on equity, or surplus. Therefore, ALM can be defined as the structuring and management of a balance sheet to influence the income statement. The process has to be profit driven or it makes little sense. The first step is choosing a capital ratio, which will in turn determine the bank's leverage and required return on assets. The heart of ROA is the net interest margin; therefore, ALM requires the proper selection of earning assets, and the optimal mix of liabilities. The mechanics of ALM can be very sophisticated or relatively simple, as long as management is focusing on the key goals and strategies.

J. J. Clarke, Ph.D
Villanova University

■ The most critical ingredients for successful balance sheet management are a well-educated and informed management team and a well-designed, concise asset/liability reporting package.

George Darling
Darling Consulting Group

■ A/L management, long-range planning, and the budgeting process are all fundamental components of any financial institution's financial management process. With the complexities of new financial instruments, fluctuating interest rates, and increased competition, these management processes become vital for the future success of the industry itself. In the past, traditional A/L management has only focused on satisfying minimum examination requirements which typically measure "current strategic position." In the Nineties, successful A/L management should also test the "future strategic direction" of the organization. Just satisfying examination requirements isn't good enough—upper management must make successful implementation of the complete A/L process imperative to survive and prosper.

Robert C. Goedken, Vice President
Profitstar, Inc.

■ Anything that you can do with traditional, spot market instruments, you can probably do with derivative products, either for a cheaper cost or a more attractive return.

Derivative markets tend to be attractive surrogates for virtually any kind of a cash market instrument. Specifically with regard to derivatives in the form of futures and exchange-traded options, the concentration of trading activity fosters narrow bid/ask spreads and low transaction costs, which in turn result in enhanced performance. To be fair, part of the "cost" of using derivative markets is the investment in human capital required to achieve the prerequisite knowledge base for the financial manager. But given the ongoing availability of incremental benefits from these instruments, it seems likely that the prospective payoff from the investment in time and effort will justify the effort for virtually every significant financial organization that expects to endure.

Ira G. Kawaller, Vice President
Chicago Mercantile Exchange

■ If you want to have a successful asset/liability management process, simply remember to have a cup of TEA:

1. **Thought.** The thought processes and methodologies underpinning your risk measurement system must be conceptually sound. Moreover, the analyses produced should help clarify the key issues so management can be focused on making the appropriate decisions. You have to know precisely what you want to accomplish.

2. **Emotion.** As the asset/liability manager, you will likely be one of the few people within your institution that fully understands the intricacies of risk management. Therefore, you must be passionate about your work and persuasive about your conclusions so as to get the key decision makers fully on board and committed to the overall asset/liability program. You need to be 100% committed to achieving your goals.

3. **Action.** Without action, even world-class analysis is reduced to a valueless intellectual exercise. Thus, the real question is not "What if?", it is "So what?" What are you going to do to improve risk-adjusted returns of your institution? You have to take action.

While the above may sound simple, it is a discipline that is the key to success in asset/liability management and nearly all of life's pursuits. So at your next ALCO meeting, make sure TEA is served.

James C. Lam, Senior Consultant
First Manhattan Consulting Group

■ Over the past decade, a lot of thought, labor, and dollars have gone into the effort of reducing the complex reality of commercial banking to a two-dimensional spreadsheet. The effort has been outstandingly successful. Today, the GAP report reigns supreme in the kingdom of banking.

Over that same span of years, the banking system has steadily lost customers; first borrowers, then depositors. Today, the realm seems diminished in both wealth and importance.

What possible connection might there be between these two developments? Maybe bankers shy away from booking hard-to-categorize business: assets with longer maturities than the GAP report allows; liabilities with uncertain durations; balance sheet products with imbedded options; investments with relatively low current yields, but great potential for future appreciation. Maybe we've been running our banks to suit the model, rather than the other way around. To the degree this is so, is it any wonder we have fewer customers?

John Ward Logan
First American National Bank

■ The most important aspect of asset/liability management is the ability to create a focused, results-oriented process. Too many managers enter an A/L meeting confronted with reams of useless and confusing data. The key is to develop a package which clearly defines their liquidity, interest rate risk, and capital position, so that senior management and the Board of Directors can make informed decisions. I recall speaking with a bank president prior to a seminar we were conducting for his institution. When asked how we could provide the maximum educational value to his senior management and board, his response was "Baby food . . . I want it to be digested like baby food!"

Brian J. McNiff, Product Manager
SunGard Financial Systems

■ A bank's three major risks are interest rate risk, liquidity risk and credit risk. Safe and sound recognition and management of interest rate risk requires people with appropriate experience and knowhow. Your success in avoiding interest rate risk ignorance is a function of the people involved in the A/L process. You can have a fine simulation model, but without appropriately experienced people who clearly understand what they are supposed to do, interest rate risk ignorance is an invitation to insolvency. Would you assign a person inexperienced in lending to be your senior lending officer?

Deedee Myers, Vice President
Myers-Kohl Corp.

■ A/L Management often receives inadequate and ineffective management attention because it quickly develops into an esoteric analytical discipline addressing the most theoretically elegant measurement of interest rate risk. More properly positioned, A/L Management should be defined and addressed as the discipline of establishing *active management control over net interest margin*. As such, it represents one of the greatest profit improvement opportunities facing any financial institution.

John C. Dorman, President
Treasury Services Corp.

■ It is important to remember that asset/liability management is an art that deals with handling uncertainty. None of us can predict future rates, prepayments, defaults, volumes, spreads, etc. with great confidence and so the thrust of our efforts should be not upon forecasting specific income or market values but rather upon quantifying the ranges within which these entities may fall, that is, the focus should be upon quantifying future exposures. Then the task is to point your institution in the general direction (pricing, volume, hedging) that fits management's risk/return preferences. The direction, of course, is more specific in the short term and becomes more general further out in time.

This focus implies not getting overly concerned with the accuracy of data of your current book (uncertainty in future overwhelms accuracy of data in the present) and it implies having some sort of presentation vehicle, risk return matrices, graphs, etc., that concisely displays future exposures for management's review.

Mel Strauss, Vice President
Chase Financial Technologies
Chase Manhattan Bank

■ Vining-Sparks' approach to asset/liability management involves analyzing a bank's income statement gap. This approach measures the price sensitivity of categories of assets and liabilities under different interest rate scenarios. This method operates under the assumption that interest rates on different groups of assets and liabilities do not change by the same amount. Forecasting actual planned changes in loan and investment yields by category and deposit rates by category will provide a better measure of the effect of changing rates on net interest margin. This is the purpose of an income statement gap.

Jim Vining, President
Vining-Sparks, IBG

■ It should be remembered that measuring interest rate risk is an art, as opposed to a science. As such, no single approach can be applied unilaterally to all financial institutions without the application of common sense. Each local market has different economic risks and therefore different responses to changing interest rates. Even though the tools for measuring a balance sheet's inherent interest rate risk are constantly evolving, they must be utilized to augment the practical application of an asset/liability manager's intuitive knowledge of his local marketplace.

Randy Wade, Senior Vice President
Vining-Sparks IBG

■ An effective asset/liability management process incorporates many components, one of which is a simulation model. The simulation process must divide asset/liability management into manageable parts. These parts often come from incompatible subsystems managed by separate units within an institution. Different tools, such as gap, simulations, market value and duration are used to analyze these components.

A good simulation model will follow an organized plan and allow separate components to be isolated and analyzed individually. For example, the planning phase differs from the analysis phase; historical data are used in some calculations, future projections in others; balance sheet changes can be immediate or gradual. Finally, the presentation of results to decision makers must contain just the right amount of meaningful data in a readily understandable form.

The key to successful planning within a financial institution is the organization of the asset/liability management process so that the results promote sound business decisions.

Geoffrey Webb, Ph.D
The Sendero Institute

■ What is all this noise about asset/liability management anyway? Is it a beleaguered industry's response to a well-intended but misguided set of directives from its regulators? Is it the theoretical but physically impractical quantitative gyrations of a set of frustrated financial analysts? Or is it simply a cynical plot on the part of software developers and PC providers to sell overly complex systems to understaffed and overburdened financial managers?

On the surface, it seems that all the talk about A/LM is nothing more than gibberish. But on closer examination, we find that there is value in the process, if properly implemented and adequately maintained. The key, of course, is that A/LM must be viewed as a process, not simply a set of disconnected analyses done in a vacuum to satisfy some distant regulatory requirement.

This one concept is critical to maximizing the benefit received from all of the efforts required to make the process work. A/LM is different from the more traditional financial accounting functions in that it involves the process of managing, as opposed to operating, the institution. The production of reports and analyses should be viewed as the beginning of the A/LM process, not the end objective. Anyone in the organization can use them as road maps to tell where the institution has been and which direction to turn in the future.

In the final analysis, A/LM is an integral part of the management of a financial institution. There is no substitute for it, and its primary responsibilities cannot be delegated away to lower level functionaries. It is perhaps the single most important process that senior managers should drive on their way to continually improving the performance of their organizations.

Jerry Weiner, President
Interactive Planning Systems, Inc.

■ Managing interest rate risk is an art and a science. But without the science (that is, measurement), it is impossible to practice the art. Some suggestions:

- ■ Manage both market value and earnings volatility and decide how you will trade them off.
- ■ Focus on the assumptions you make about hard-to-understand assets and liabilities (e.g., demand deposits, reserves, and other non–interest bearing assets and liabilities). Make informed judgments based on thorough analyses of the pertinent assets or liabilities.
- ■ Identify and quantify (wherever possible) basis risks and option risks. Reflect them in your reports, interpretations of reports, and actions.
- ■ Measure results. How much market value and earnings did you create (or destroy), when calling rate movements, selecting attractive spread discretionary assets, managing basis risk, or taking options risk?

Ken Westerbeck
LaSalle National Bank

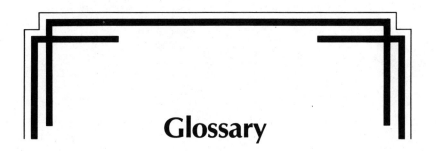

Glossary

Glossary

ALCO   Acronym for asset/liability committee.

ARM   Acronym for adjustable-rate mortage.

Asset/liability management   The process of planning, directing, and controlling the flow, level, mix, cost, yield, and duration of funds for the purposes of achieving financial goals and controlling financial risks.

Arbitrage   Funding an earning asset by using lower-costing funds such that a positive interest rate spread is produced.

Asset utilization   Total gross income divided by average total net assets.

Basis point   1/100 of 1% or .01% or .0001.

Basis risk   The risk in an arbitrage that the rate being paid on the funding liability will change by a different amount than the rate being received on the earning asset.

Cap   A contract between two parties based on a notional amount under which the buyer pays the seller a fee in exchange for the right to receive the difference between the base rate stated in the contract and the current market rate when the current market rate exceeds the stated rate.

Capital multiplier   Average total assets dividend by average total capital.

Computer simulation   A way to measure financial risks using a computer model to forecast the impact a change in interest rates will have on an institution's net income and net value of portfolio equity.

Convexity   The measure of how much a price/yield curve deviates from a straight line.

Costing liabilities   The dollar amount of liabilities for which the firm pays explicit interest.

Credit risk   The possibility that a loan or investment will not be repaid as originally agreed.

Cross Hedge   Hedging the interest rate risk of one instrument such as prime rate based loans with a synthetic instrument based on another interest rate such as a futures contract using the 91 day Treasury bill rate.

Dependency Ratio   Potentially volatile liabilities (i.e. brokered deposits, time deposits $100,000 and over) minus short-term investments divided by total earning assets minus short term investments. The higher this ratio, the greater the potential for a liquidity problem.

Download   The act of transferring data from one computer to another.

Disintermediation   The act of withdrawing deposits from a financial institution and using the funds to purchase higher yielding investment instruments.

Driver rate   An interest rate used by a simulation model to affect other interest rates. For example, if the one-year Treasury bill rate is the driver rate for one-year CDs and one-year ARMs, an increase in the one-year Treasury bill rate will automatically increase the one-year CD rate and the one-year ARM rate.

Duration   The time-weighted, present-valued average maturity of the cash flows of a financial instrument.

Dynamic gap   The bank's gap position viewed over several different time periods.

Earning assets   Interest-earning assets including loans, investment securities, leases and federal funds sold. The sum of all assets that earn interest.

Earning asset ratio   The ratio of total earning assets divided by total assets.

Equity multiplier   The dollar amount of assets being supported by each dollar of capital. It is calculated by dividing total assets by total equity.

Financial futures contract   A commitment between two parties to purchase (sell) a stated quantity of a financial asset on a future specified date at a specified price.

Floor   A contract between two parties based on a notional amount under which the buyer pays the seller a fee in exchange for the right to receive the difference between the base rate stated in the contract and the current market rate when the current market rate is less than the stated rate.

Gap   The difference between rate-sensitive assets and rate-sensitive liabilities.

Goal   A statement of what an institution proposes to accomplish.

HLT   Acronym for highly leveraged transaction.

Interest rate risk   The possibility that a change in interest rates will adversely impact either the net income or the value of a firm.

LIBOR   Acronym for London Inter Bank Offered Rate. A widely publicized rate at which European banks lend to each other.

Liquidity risk   The possibility that an institution will have inadequate funds to meet the legitimate demands for cash by its depositors and lenders.

Market value of portfolio equity (Also referred to as Net value of portfolio equity)   The difference between the net present value of an institution's assets and the net present value of its liabilities.

Matched funding   The process of pairing off the various components of a bank's balance sheet as each asset category is being funded by a specific liability category.

Mix   The proportional composition of the various components of assets and liabilities.

Net duration analysis   Duration of the equity position is determined by the net duration of the assets and the liabilities.

Net interest income   The difference between total interest income and total interest expense.

Net interest margin   The difference between the average interest rate received on the assets and the average interest rate paid on the liabilities.

Net interest position   The amount by which earning assets exceed interest bearing liabilities.

Net interest spread   The interest yield on earning assets less the interest cost of the liabilities.

Net noninterest nonoperating margin Noninterest nonoperating income (i.e. securties gains/losses, extraordinary items) less noninterest nonoperating expense (i.e. provision for loan losses, extraordinary items) divided by average total assets.

Net noninterest operating margin Noninterest operating income less noninterest operating expenses divided by average total assets.

Net present value The dollar difference between the present value of expected cash inflows and the present value of expected cash outflows.

Net present value analysis A measure of the net present value of the cash flows from assets and liabilities under various interest rate scenarios.

Noninterest income All income other than interest on loans and investments.

Notional amount A principal amount used when computing the interest payments on swaps, caps, and floors.

Profit margin Net income after taxes divided by total gross income.

Rate-sensitive assets Assets with either a short-term maturity (variously defined from one day to one year) or with a variable or floating interest rate.

Rate-sensitive liabilities Liabilities with either a short-term maturity (variously defined from one day to one year) or with a variable or floating interest rate.

Repurchase Agreement (Repo) A short term investment alternative. The opposite of a reverse repurchase agreement. A financial institution enters into an agreement with another party (usually a securities dealer) in which the institution buys a security from the dealer and simultaneously agrees to sell the security back to the dealer at a stated future date for a slightly higher price. The price differential is the equivalent to an interest rate that is usually slightly less than the Federal funds rate and constitutes the return on the transaction.

Return on assets (ROA)   Net income divided by average total assets.

Return on earning assets   Net income divided by average earnings assets.

Return on equity (ROE)   Net income divided by average equity capital.

Reverse Repurchase Agreement (Reverse Repo)   A method of borrowing funds. The opposite of a repurchase agreement. A financial institution enters into an agreement with another party (usually a securities dealer) in which the institution sells a security to the dealer and simultaneously agrees to repurchase the security at a stated future date for a slightly higher price. The price differential is the equivalent to an interest rate that is usually slightly less than the Federal funds rate and constitutes the cost of borrowing the funds.

Short-term liquidity requirement   Liquidity demand resulting from daily fluctuations in the balance sheet.

Structural liquidity requirement   Long-term or permanent changes in a balance sheet's structure that creates a demand for liquidity.

Seasonal liquidity requirement   Liquidity need arising from seasonal changes in the balance sheet structure.

Static gap   The bank's gap position at a single point in time.

Swap   A contract based on a notional amount, under which one party agrees to receive a fixed rate of interest for a stated period of time and pay the other party a variable rate of interest for the same time period.

Synthetic instrument   An interest rate contract such as a swap, cap, or floor.

What-if scenario   A hypothetical interest rate scenario in which the bank's performance is tested using a modeling system.

Yield curve risk   The risk to the net interest margin that can occur with a change in the shape of the yield curve.

Index

Index

272